Compassion: Our last great hope

A Tribute

Leo K. Bustad with Johnny Jump-Up, his wife Signe's hearing dog.

To honor Leo K. Bustad, D.V.M., Ph.D., for his great compassion, dynamic leadership, and pioneering role in forging new partnerships between people, animals and the natural environment, the first edition of this book was published in 1990 when Delta Society presented to Dr. Bustad the Distinguished Service Award.

The second edition is offered as a continuing tribute to this remarkable man.

Thanks to the generous support of Hill's Pet Nutrition, Inc., the proceeds from the sale of this book will be donated to Delta Society and People-Pet Partnership to continue his work.

Selected Speeches of Leo K. Bustad, D.V.M., Ph.D.

Published by Delta Society

Compassion: Our last great hope

Grateful acknowledgment for permission to
reprint previously published material is made to
National Forum for excerpts from the article "More
Than Scholars;" to *Trends* for excerpts from the
article "The Importance of Animals to the Well-
Being of People;" to Charles C. Thomas for
excerpts from *Interrelations Between People and Pets* in
"Concern for Children;" to Random House, Inc.
for excerpts from *Sophie's Choice* by William Styron
in "Holocausts" and "Grief;" to Plenum Press for
excerpts from *Swine in Biomedical Research* in "Pigs:
From BC-2,000 AD;" to W.W. Norton & Company,
Inc. for excerpts from *Eleanor and Franklin* by
Joseph P. Lash (© 1971 by Joseph R. Lash) in
"Compassion: Our Last Great Hope;" to
HarperCollins Publishers Inc. for quotations from
*A Spirituality Named Compassion and the Healing of the
Global Village, Humpty Dumpty and Us* by Matthew
Fox (© 1979 by Matthew Fox) in "Compassion:
Our Last Great Hope;" and to *Anthrozoös* for
excerpts from the editorials by Andrew Rowan
"Our Responsibilities to the Natural World" and
"The Power of the Telling Anecdote."

Dedication

To the growing number of people who appreciate, recognize, and respect the capabilities of animals and diligently contribute to their care, well-being and improved habitat. To my dear friend, the late Dean Hy Kitchen of the University of Tennessee, who was a committed, compassionate leader in this rewarding effort.

To those who work diligently in selecting and training animals as assistants and for involvement in animal-assisted therapy and who insure that the animals' well-being is maintained and their lives enriched.

To all the animals who have contributed and are contributing to the happiness, health and well-being of people, especially those with disabilities, e.g., Signe's hearing dogs Bridget and Johnny and the dogs trained by prisoners at the Washington Correction Center for Women, who detect impending seizures before their owners recognize them and thereby have changed their lives in a remarkable way.

To my wife, Signe, for being my hands and feet, my head and heart, for over 50 years, in spite of much adversity, including cancer.

To our son, Buzz, and our daughter Becky for their compassionate concern for animals.

To our daughter Karen, who died in Cameroon, West Africa, after two years of effective volunteer service there. We are comforted to know that so many people—most especially children and the young in heart—were singularly blessed by Karen's life; and that her great love for animals moved her to raise the sensitivity of the people she worked with regarding their care and concern for animals.

Hail to all compassionate nurturers!

Do not grow weary in well doing!

Onward and Upward!

Table of Contents

Foreword

The first time I heard Leo Bustad speak was in Vancouver in 1979 at a meeting called Pets in Society. The memory is as clear as quartz because I recall mumbling almost out loud, "WHO IS THIS MAN?" I was in the midst of planning an international meeting to be held the next year in London to be called the Human-Companion Animal Bond and was there to hear what was going on in Canada. Leo was there to explain to the Canadians the People-Pet Partnership then in its infancy at Washington State University.

Leo was introduced as the dean of the veterinary college at Pullman, a career scientist with a long background in nuclear medicine. He didn't look like the East Coast deans I had met or had listened to; actually more like Ichabod Crane, but I put that down to the cultural differences that the Rockies create. I settled into my chair as best I could and awaited what I thought was going to be a set-piece, "This is what we're doing at my college," talk.

Standing angular at the podium, peering over his half glasses, he called for the lights to be dimmed and started talking. Leo explained he was from Pullman and showed us a slide of that remote part of eastern Washington State. "It's not the end of the world," he explained as we looked at the barren landscape and he paused, and then leaning slightly forward and squinting at us, continued, "but you can see it from there."

I sat bolt upright. "WHO IS THIS MAN?" No veterinary dean can pause like that. Leo continued. In his drawl that sounds like a cross between Jimmy Stewart and a fire and brimstone preacher, he described his interest in the role of pets in society and explained that he enjoys the companionship of a dog. Up came a slide of Leo in a running position behind a parked Volkswagen, holding a geriatric dog in his arms. PAUSE......Lean forward. Squint. "My dog's old but she still likes to chase cars."

Leo continued to describe Pullman and its veterinary curriculum. He explained how the curriculum committee operates and, teasingly, told a story of the Paleolithic university where students are taught to catch salmon with their bare hands. A new member of the faculty, a bright spark, tells them he has a new idea. "There's this thing I call a spear," he says, "and it makes it easier to catch fish. You wait till they swim by and you spear 'em. Let's change our curriculum and teach our students to catch fish by spearing them."

The curriculum committee pondered, said Leo. Some were against the idea because "the old method worked." Others wanted to see the statistical evidence that the new technique had been tested under controlled conditions. So to solve the problem the curriculum committee set up a subcommittee to look into the matter. PAUSE ... hunch forward... squint.

Now Leo was into the meat of his talk. He explained how and why the People-Pet Partnership was set up, how it operates, who is involved and what are its objectives. You could have heard a pin drop. Like the best of fishermen, he had all us fish hooked.

I didn't meet Leo again until the following January 1980, when he attended The Human-Companion Animal Bond symposium in London. "Bruce," he said, "I'd like to introduce you to Babs Wright." Twenty-four hours in London and he was introducing a Londoner, Lady Wright, to another Londoner, me. But it wasn't just an off-chance introduction. Leo's nose for people is uncanny, and as I was to discover over the next decade almost everything Leo does has a serious purpose. Babs was the vice-chairman of the Royal National Institute for the Deaf, and I was being set up to help her create a Hearing Dogs for the Deaf scheme in Britain, now the largest in the world.

Leo and I continued to meet almost yearly throughout the eighties when he spoke in Philadelphia, New York, Boston, Houston, Vienna and many more times in London. And how well he spoke. In London he had the avuncular British veterinary profession crying for more. No one could quite believe that he was a veterinarian let alone that he was a dean of an American veterinary school. How could a veterinarian, how could an academic have so much PASSION?

The passion is there only for those of us who have been fortunate enough to listen to Leo speak or for those of us who have had the opportunity to become his friends. But his influence on attitudes toward companion animals reaches a far wider audience. No one has done more to teach us our responsibilities toward animals.

I'm one of the few people amongst my friends and relatives who still has both his parents alive and healthy. Both have always been rewarding. But even in those happy circumstances, it's still possible to have another kind of father figure and that's what Leo is. To use one of his (and now my) favorite words, he's a "serendipitous" father figure, a happy chance. Leo's gift is to teach with enthusiasm, to convince with humor, to articulate with wit. Not many of us ever have the chance to meet individuals who are so gifted let alone to strike a friendship with them. Opportunities such as that can change your life and Leo has had that influence on many more people than me alone. Enjoy reading this book. Leo's thoughts and sentiments, at one time lightly considered by the scientific educational establishment, are now major themes in humane education. Enjoy reading but remember, your pleasure is only a fraction of what it would be by being in the same room as this marvelous man.

Bruce Fogle, DVM, MRCVS
London, England

People most worth encountering tend to jolt you out of your habitual, pre-conceived and stereotyped way of doing and seeing things and help you see a new self, or a new world. The best of these remarkable people make those kinds of transformations "with the grain"—without your awareness of how it is being done. With Leo Bustad's lectures, the enlightenment takes place under the cover of charm, laughter, and that rarest of qualities: an *open-minded* moral conviction. Leo's talks are like an introduction to a family at some kind of festive gathering. There are jokes, a kind of avuncular narration—an intimation that new wisdom might be derived from the application of very old wisdom, a sense of goodwill that has a penumbra of moral fervor; just a hint of a preachment.

The first time I heard Leo—in London at the companion animal meeting chaired by Bruce Fogle—my first response was mild affront. Research was not talked that way. I knew he was a well-respected scientist but wondered why he was presenting information about human-animal relationships like he was toast-master at someone's golden wedding anniversary. I was also aware of a growing apprehension. I had to follow him on the program, and I sensed that he was transforming my audience from a group of individuals into a community or a family. Knowledge of that transformation offered me a choice. I could remain outside by insisting on a strict separation between the realm of fact: statements that I could prove or disprove by employing the formal rules of research, or I could join the gathering by entering the less perfect domain of human dialogue where fact had to be joined to feeling, poetry, moral principle and a pervasive empathy for living things. There was no real choice. The reader of these essays should be warned that Leo's humor is like bait on a hook, designed to fish for people who can take on his tasks. In another sense, the humor is a beacon trans-mitting the real messages: celebration of life, reverence for life, a way of being in which your feelings, your science, your moral sense, all begin to work togeth-er to restore a sense of wholeness and purpose. An apprehension achieved through the recognition that we are inextricably joined to all the other kinds of living beings who share our world.

Unfortunately, these talks must be read without the immediate presence of the person who wrote them. They are a kind of envelope, or Kirlian photograph, indicating the absent person of their author. They are, in many respects, like an album of family photographs, and must be read as an introduction to a family; the family Leo created within the Delta Society. Like family albums, they may be read for instruction and remembrance, but their real purpose is to welcome new members. Leo has tirelessly weaved his way about the world gathering in people by ones and twos, tens and hundreds. This volume should be used in the same way. It should not rest on a shelf. It should circulate, doing Leo's kind of work, welcoming new people into the fold. The owners of this volume, many of whom can supplement it with their own experience with Leo in action, should accom-pany the book, adding their own welcome to those contained in these pages.

Family albums serve another purpose; they keep the memory and the spirit of those we have lost in our present and our presence. Leo's discourse keeps peo-ple with us and commits us to sharing their purpose. Michael McCulloch, Konrad Lorenz, Boris Levinson, Ange Condoret, and R. Stirling Hogarth-Scott animate these pages as vividly as those who are still carrying on their work. In this sense, Leo's volume of talks carries on a dialogue for others. But that is the real purpose of the Delta Society. Its members must speak for those in the community of living beings who can no longer speak, or who could never speak. Our community contains all of the animals who speak to us through Leo Bustad's discourse, a continuing dialogue which reminds us that to live in the company of animals is an enormous but endangered privilege, a privilege that we must strive to preserve.

Aaron Katcher, MD
Philadelphia, PA

Acknowledgements
(and Apologies)

I am grateful for all the people whose writings or presentations have helped me so much throughout my life. I have tried to give credit to those whose work I've incorporated, but I have failed to find some sources. Giving proper credit is a real concern for me. In my reading and listening I've made many notes and have been sponge-like on hearing discourse, especially on issues that are of special interest to me; however, the source wasn't always identified. Now after all these years and memory loss, it is difficult to establish the true source of an idea or quotation. In some cases I have modified part of a presentation or idea and added some new "wrinkles." I know in some cases the initial kernel of the idea wasn't mine, but the person who could provide attribution has died. Others have failed to respond to inquiry. I hope those not identified or given appropriate credit will inform me of the use of their material, as well as feel complimented that I've incorporated their views in a philosophy for our time.

If I were to list all the people who have contributed in a meaningful way to my life as reflected in the presentations in this book, there would be no room for the presentations. But the book would probably be more interesting. In addition to all the people referred to in the text, I was fortunate in having outstanding advisors, mentors and associates in my professional, post-professional and graduate studies and activities including: Loren Carlson, Lauren Donaldson and Orville Smith at the University of Washington; Tony Cunha and M.E. Ensminger at Washington State University; Shields Warren at Harvard; my fellow deans at WSU and in veterinary medicine schools throughout the world; Linda Hines and the Board of Directors of Delta Society and friends of this society here and throughout the world. I am also indebted to Dame Phyllis Frost, Jean Hampl, Virginia Walster, Mary Whyham, Paul Walsh and Don Verlander for their important contributions.

This second edition has been edited by Mary Jane Engh, with expert counsel provided by Linda Hines, Executive Director, Delta Society. I am furthermore grateful for assistance provided by Ruth Landau, and by staff at the Washington State University College of Veterinary Medicine. Special gratitude goes to Sancho for his continuing interest in and creative contributions to our program, including gifts of his original artworks, one of which appears on the cover of this book. Finally, my thanks to Andrea Ptak for critical work in layout and preparing this volume for printing.

Introduction

"Comedy is simply a funny way of being serious." — Peter Ustinov.

As I approached my 70th birthday, my ability to perform at a "high lope" and cope with stress was obviously deteriorating, and I began to say no to many invitations. On returning from the Fifth International Conference on the Relationship Between Humans and Animals in Monaco in November 1989, I was in ill health so I canceled all out-of-state commitments for the foreseeable future. In response to many inquiries, I sent out a letter thanking people for their concern. I told them I consider it miraculous that I made it to the age of three score and ten—when I didn't expect to make it to one score and four. Although it's very difficult for one with Nordic blood and genes to admit to vulnerability, the slings and arrows of aging, World War II and prison camp, and a host of other adversities have taken their toll. Continuous headaches and dizziness have caused me to have my head examined—something countless numbers of people have recommended most of my life. I've become philosophical about my situation as I recall part of the haunting refrain of "September Song" (Anderson, 1938):

> Oh, it's a long, long while from May to December,
> But the days grow short when you reach September.
> When the autumn weather turns the leaves to flame....
> Oh, the days dwindle down to a precious few,
> September, November!

When my associates decided to have a book of my papers published, they suggested I give a bit of my history, especially that which might bear directly or indirectly on the subjects of the presentations in this book. The following is a historical perspective of those events that I felt shaped my character (or made me a character), and ideals that led me into the fascinating and rewarding arena of the interdependency of people, animals and the environment.

I was born at a very tender age in a small house in the Scandinavian farming community of Stanwood in Western Washington. I had an older brother, John, and younger sister, Romola. My folks were Norwegian immigrants, and Norwegian was my first language. When my brother started school, we began talking more English at home. When I was ten my grandmother, who could not speak English, died. Thereafter I had few occasions to speak Norwegian and, unfortunately, forgot much of it (but never my compassionate grandmother).

My early life was a busy and interesting one. We had cats, dairy cows, chickens and sometimes turkeys (including a gobbler who threatened me), a pig or two and, for a time, a goat. There were woods to play in, and a creek to fish in and fall into. One neighbor had ducks and guinea hens, and another had horses, a lot of machinery and the first radio set (a crystal set). I'd sit on the lap of that neighbor, Conrad, as he'd tune in a station for me to listen to which was predominantly static—but interesting static.

I still vividly recall three traumatic events in my first six years. When I was less than four years old, my brother encouraged me to run through a bunch of dried ferns that my father had burned. There were sufficient burning embers remaining, so I caught on fire. My father, I believe, was burned more seriously than I, although I still carry a scar. The second event was more serious. When I was about four years old and lying on the floor by our wood cook stove, my aunt removed a large kettle of boiling water from the stove and accidentally spilled it all on my back. A far bigger scar was left, and the burn was a source of much pain for quite some time.

The third scar I carry occurred on the Fourth of July in 1926 when our family went for a ride in our new Model T Ford sedan. My mother was driving and the car went off the road in loose gravel, onto an embankment, and tipped over on my side of the car. Someone helped us tip the car back on its wheels, and we went "toodling" home—grateful there were no injuries except to my right middle finger.

Our neighbors in Stanwood were kind and very helpful, forming a true community. My first five grades were spent in a one-room school, and I was blessed with outstanding teachers. Miss Newcomb taught me the first year and Miss Larson the next four grades (which took three years since I was promoted from the third grade to the fourth grade mid-year). In the first grade, when I was recovering from a serious bout with pneumonia, Miss Newcomb came to our home and reviewed class assignments to "bring me up to speed" with my classmates.

Miss Larson was the teacher I had more association with than any other until I was in graduate school. She was like Miss Newcomb—a very caring person and an excellent teacher. In this regard both teachers showed real concern for Erling, a schoolmate who was different and picked on by some children who teased him and called him crazy. My mother and father, too, were concerned about Erling and told me I must help look after him (and all people with disabilities, as well as the elderly). This concern included going to Erling's home some Saturdays to play and inviting him to come to our house for afternoon refreshments. (It also included visiting elderly people with my mother.)

One of the many remarkable traits of these two teachers was that they kept track of me—well into my 60s, even sending a granddaughter to "check up" on me while I was dean. Thank God for such caring, compassionate teachers—may their number multiply!

There's an advantage to having many grades in one school; at least it was for me in my first five grades and also in my other schools for the sixth through the twelfth grades. Our four-year high school had only 100 students, so each student had the opportunity (and was sometimes duty bound) to participate in all kinds of activities. I was Chief of the Friendly Indian Club in sixth or seventh grade. I played trombone and baritone in the high school band for six or seven years (starting in the sixth and seventh grade). I worked on the school paper, and I was the manager for all sports activities and helped coach the "scrub" teams. This also included being scorekeeper, water boy, "medicine" man and unofficial counselor. I enjoyed my assignment except that when they won a big game, they'd throw me into the shower with my clothes on.

Many other activities rounded out my school years. I was in most of the "plays," which I won't honor by calling them theatrical productions. I was also student body president in my senior year, and I was on the animal and crop judging teams in my final year of high school when vocational agriculture was introduced. At the Future Farmers of America (FFA) annual conference at Washington State University (WSU) in 1937, two of us took first place in judging in our category. Everyone considered this to be quite an achievement for several reasons: We were representing one of the smallest schools in the state; our school was in its first year of vocational agriculture; and our teacher was in his first year of teaching. Our hometown had a banquet in honor of our judging team, our program and our teacher, who convinced two of us to enroll as freshmen at WSU. My goal was to be a vocational agriculture teacher.

My first year in college was the biggest transition of my life to that point. I worked my way through college and "batched" all four years. I also enrolled in advanced ROTC (Reserve Officers Training Corps) and was involved in a number of other activities, including a year as president of the All-Ag Club. Since I was separated from all the animals at my home, it was comforting to have access to some of the herds and flocks in the College of Agriculture.

The best thing that happened to me in college was that I met my future wife, Signe Byrd, there. She was a classmate majoring in Home Economics.

On graduation day, June 9, 1941, I received not only my diploma, but my appointment as a second lieutenant in the Reserve Officers Corps and orders to report the next day for active duty at Fort George Wright in Spokane, Washington. I was stationed at Fort Lewis, Washington, when the Japanese attacked Pearl Harbor on December 7, 1941. On that Sunday I was invited to have dinner with Signe at her folks' home in Tacoma. It was there we heard the news and the order for all military personnel to return to their bases. It was a very frightening time. Almost all military personnel left the Fort and set up camp in the forest some distance away in case the Fort was attacked. However, since I had broken my wrist, I was ordered to stay with a skeleton force at the Fort.

Until the time of this attack (and for several years before) people my age were very apprehensive about the future. We wondered—would the United States become actively engaged in the war? On that fateful Sunday we had our answer, and it wasn't the one we wanted. We knew then that we were in for a long war, and we realized we might be killed or injured entering into infantry combat early in the war. We cited figures of the average life of lieutenants in combat, and it was a sobering figure—measured in minutes, not hours. But that didn't prevent Signe from joining me in Georgia at the Fort Benning chapel on June 13, 1942, to be married. She had just finished her first year of teaching, and I was at Fort Benning attending Communication Officers School.

After the Japanese attack we started practicing beach landings to prepare to retake land lost in Africa, Europe and the South Pacific to Germany and Japan. We were scheduled for duty in the South Pacific, but plans were changed and we went to Virginia to prepare for the invasion in Africa. Just before embarking at Newport News, Virginia, some of us were called in for a briefing by the commander of the invasion forces, General George Patton. He was impressive in his impeccable uniform complete with pearl-handled pistols. It was the first briefing I'd ever attended in which every three words or so were punctuated by obscenities.

Following our briefing with Patton, we were launched for a trip across the Atlantic which was populated by German submarines, some of which followed us. Before leaving, I bade a sad farewell to my wife whom I wouldn't see again for 32 months. When we had crossed the Atlantic and reached the African coast and our assigned launching point (where we were to leave the troop ship for small landing craft), it was about two o'clock in the morning. Although we had blackout conditions, we had a radio receiver on and were shocked to hear President Roosevelt come on the air to announce that American forces were landing on the shores of North Africa. It was many hours before our assault troops were scheduled to land! Apparently someone didn't know the correct time difference between Eastern Standard Time and Moroccan Time. It was supposed to be a secret mission until we landed, but when you stop and think about it, the operation was not a secret to the Germans who had tracked us. It was only a secret to the American people. The coastal gun batteries fired on us but were soon silenced by the cruiser Augusta.

The landing was successful with a minimal loss of life, but there were many anxious moments as we quickly advanced to capture our assigned objective, Casablanca—a beautiful city. The capture was accomplished within three days. Although it was new territory for all of us, landing where we did was about like landing in our own backyard because we had memorized the terrain from maps and pictures available to us long before the landing.

One of the most memorable aspects of the landing to me was a local farmer who was plowing a field with a donkey paired with a camel. Even with all the activity, he appeared oblivious to what was occurring around him. Another memorable item was our experience in trying to establish communications with the advancing troops and with our rear echelon. As fast as we laid wire for our telephone hookup, local people would roll the wire back up and disappear with it.

To be successful in a campaign is an exhilarating experience, as I realized when we captured Casablanca. But the big cost was the loss of several good friends, including my best friend, Lambert. It is well that I didn't know then how many more battles I'd have to fight and how many more friends I'd have to lose. We were involved in the "mop up" of the German Africa Corps in Tunisia, the assault on Southern Sicily and capture of Palermo and Messina, and the invasion "in reserve" at Salerno. At that point I was ordered back to North Africa to recuperate from hepatitis, amoebic dysentery and possible malaria. I returned to make the assault landing at Anzio (the port of Rome); and then the first attempted breakthrough out of Anzio which failed, leaving me and quite a few others five miles behind enemy lines.

It was during this final mission that I was captured, and I spent the next 15 months as a prisoner of war. Chronologically, I spent time in Italy, Southern Germany and the Polish corridor. Then I traveled by foot to Northern Germany, by boxcar to Southwestern Germany, and eventually back to Southern Germany by foot where I was finally liberated for the third and last time—one of the happiest moments of my life. (I had been liberated and recaptured first on the Russian Front and second on the Western Front.) I much preferred walking rather than being locked in boxcars that were targets of our Air Force; we were, however, also bombed and strafed while walking.

I must go back and relate one (of many) of my close calls. We were in ships in a large convoy from Africa, and the day before the Sicilian invasion a terrible storm blew up with 50- to 60-mile-an-hour winds. During this storm I was washed overboard and my life belt was inoperative. I fortunately caught a "donut" life preserver and for the next 45 minutes floated the Mediterranean—hoping for rescue. The last ship in our convoy was Landing Craft Infantry (LCI) -13 which missed picking me up as it passed by; against standing orders the captain turned the ship around and tried to rescue me again. Failing, he then decided he'd go on the windward side and either hit me or rescue me. Obviously he succeeded in rescuing me. Since the storm was so severe, they couldn't transfer me to the command vessel I had been on. The next morning on landing in Southern Sicily, the command vessel I was unable to return to was hit by gunfire, killing 11 of my associates.

Some of my experiences in prison still haunt me and I prefer not to recall them, but a few incidents appear in this book. It was a tremendous learning experience; it was interesting and often disheartening to see how people reacted to great adversity. An important void in prison camp life was a complete lack of association with animals. I'll admit, however, I had close attachment to fleas, lice and bedbugs, but that was not a healthy human-animal bond. Cold and hunger also left their marks on me. I swore I'd never be cold again—so I overdress. Sometimes I even wear long johns in June. And I'm never without a food supply near at hand.

Prison camp life did, however, provide time for me to think about what I might do with my life if I survived. I was inclined towards medicine and animals and/or the plant sciences—but a moving force within me was the desire to control disease and promote health and well-being in living things. Adversity is a severe, but effective, teacher. Had I not been a prisoner I probably would not now be as involved as I am with Habitat for Humanity, Bread for the World, Amnesty International, animals in prison and concern especially for the plight of children and people with disabilities.

I returned to New York City on June 13, 1945, in time to call my wife on our third wedding anniversary. Homecomings involving wife and family (including animals) and friends are glorious experiences and mine was no exception. I had 65 days at home to recover and think about my future. After two months of enjoying life, my wife and I reported to an army redistribution center in beautiful Santa Barbara, California, where I was discharged.

After discharge we went by our alma mater (WSU) to talk to the dean of the College of Veterinary Medicine. After examining my records, he told me I was in the class that was to start in a few weeks. While in veterinary school I also worked on a master's degree in nutrition, a special interest of mine. My principal study was pig nutrition (vitamin requirements and causes of infant mortality) with the objective of helping pigs and people.

While I was in veterinary school, two of our three children were born. Our son, Buzz, was born in my first year and daughter Karen joined us during my last year. When Buzz was old enough to appreciate animals, we would take him to the veterinary clinic and to the farm flocks. Following my graduation from veterinary school we moved into our first house, and shortly thereafter Becky was born.

Animals were constant companions and a continual source of fun and learning for my family (we have kept pets in our family continuously for more than 50 years). Buzz once expressed an interest in having pet rats and a friend gave us two young males. The night the rats arrived it took a great effort to convince him to go to bed. His prayer that evening was especially fervent as he prayed that God would bless Mother and Dad and Karen and Becky and then, "Don't ever let anything happen to those two rats. Amen." But something did happen—one of the "male" rats gave birth. On some Sundays I'd take the children to see our sheep flock, especially during lambing season. When our children left home and set up housekeeping, they also obtained pets. (Becky chose a guinea pig—Miss Piggy—for her special education class.)

For the next 16 years, except for time out to earn a Ph.D. in mammalian physiology at the University of Washington School of Medicine, I performed and directed studies principally on sheep and pigs to learn how to live safely in the nuclear age. This was done as an employee of General Electric and later Battelle Pacific Northwest Laboratory at Richland, Washington. I then joined the University of California at Davis where I directed two laboratories as a professor in the Schools of Medicine and Veterinary Medicine.

My duties required much traveling which was somewhat distressing for Signe, so we found a small frisky terrier-type dog for her which she named Charlie. But I changed his name to Great Reluctance so that whenever I left her, I would leave her with Great Reluctance. (I was told Charles Schulz used this name in one of his *Peanuts* comic strips.)

After eight years at U.C. Davis, I was recruited to be dean of the College of Veterinary Medicine at WSU. It turned into an exciting ten years—the busiest of my life.

Many good things happened as a result of real team effort during my tenure as dean. The area that I felt had especially great potential for benefiting people and animals was something commonly referred to as the human-animal bond. I believed if we could mobilize many members of the veterinary profession, along with other health professionals and specialists in animal care and training, we could have a tremendous impact on many people—especially those who were lacking nurture and appropriate nurturing objects (which includes an ever-increasing segment of our society). We were also in need of more responsible care for animals throughout the world. We needed more reverence for life for all living things. We needed more compassion and concern!

I reached these conclusions in the early 1970s when I began investigating the impact animals have had on people for thousands of years. I visited Beitestolen in Norway in 1971 and witnessed the beneficial effects of animal interaction on people who had disabling conditions. I learned about Bethel in Germany and visited there in 1977. Bethel, an institution without walls, began in 1867 in the town of Bielefeld. Christians decided attics and back rooms were not the appropriate places to keep people with disabilities. When I visited, enlightened homelike living conditions were being provided for over 5,000 residents and about the same number of staff to care for them in a remarkable way in outstanding facilities. Animals were important members of their healing team.

In 1974 I learned that upwards of 15-18 million dogs and cats in our animal control centers were killed that year, and 80 percent of them had owners. I visited nursing homes and other institutions where animal interaction was denied. When we arrived in Pullman in 1973 we were discouraged from taking our dog into the local convalescent home. I heard complaints from many elderly people who had to give up their animals when they moved to government housing or nursing and convalescent homes where animals were not allowed. I also observed that the simple introduction of a carefully screened animal could make a remarkable change for the better in the lives of many people. And when you stop and think about it, it's understandable because a great proportion of the lives of people for thousands of years (save for the last couple of hundred) have been spent in close association with animals and the natural environment.

It was at this time that Linda Hines, now the Executive Director of the Delta Society, and I began to develop ideas for programs to facilitate human-animal interactions. Beginning in 1974 we and our associates began establishing components that would constitute the People-Pet Partnership (PPP) Program. Through PPP we developed many programs designed to enhance the human-animal interaction. A curriculum for preschool through the sixth grade was created and later published by Hill's Pet Products (now Hill's Pet Nutrition, Inc.) to provide information about types of animals, responsibilities of animal ownership and the benefits of the human-animal interaction. Guidelines were developed for placement of animals in nursing homes, and an associate, Dean Fluharty, placed kittens in a local nursing home.

Additional programs we helped initiate included an animal program in a maximum security prison for women (assisting Kathy Quinn—later Sister Pauline). With Joan Meyers and Dolly Hughes, the first university-based riding program for people with disabling conditions was started at WSU. We also designed and implemented a course at WSU entitled "Reverence for Life" (see Appendix for an outline of this course). During this time the Delta Society was established from its early status as a foundation. It has become the principal world resource and repository for information on human-animal interaction.

While the above programs were being created, we also encouraged programs to train assistance animals to help dependent people become independent. The benefits of such programs were made poignantly clear to me when my wife lost most of her hearing in 1981. She had a two-year-old dog that we rescued when we learned she was destined for the pound. We socialized her and then decided to train her as a hearing dog. Terry Ryan, an expert dog trainer and an associate, directed the dog's training with full cooperation of my wife and myself and with consultation from Sheila O'Brien at the Hearing Ear Dog Program in West Boylston, Massachusetts—now National Education for Assistance Dog Services (NEADS) in Princeton, Massachusetts. The dog was certified after a year of training and performed admirably for years. That dog, Bridget, became my wife's freedom. She and I have given many demonstrations with the dog, impressing and educating many audiences regarding the challenges of being deaf and the helpfulness of a trained dog.

The last two and a half decades have been the most rewarding of my life. I have witnessed many remarkable interactions between animals and people here in North America and in many other countries:

- To see Marie go from an unresponsive stroke victim lying in a fetal position with sores on her legs that wouldn't heal to a person not only interested in her surroundings, but responsive and enjoying life as the result of being moved into a "therapy" room with Handsome the cat.

- Or to see Angie who was born with a condition which caused frequent seizures requiring the presence of her mother or father at all times to intervene when she stopped breathing. There were times no one observed that her breathing had stopped resulting in memory loss to Angie. And then to witness the change when Sue, a prison inmate sentenced to life imprisonment, trained a dog, Sheba, to be Angie's assistant. Sheba could detect impending seizures and inform Angie when a seizure was about to occur, even before Angie was aware of it. Sheba's presence saved Angie's life several times, reduced her number of seizures, and made it possible for her to finish high school and compete successfully in the Special Olympics in gymnastics. Since Sheba, other dogs have been selected and trained by prison inmates to detect impending seizures. Such performances make a "true believer" out of one.

- And to see how another one of the dogs specially trained by Sue has changed the life of Miklos, who has quadraplegia and is unable to speak. Chance, a golden retriever, has enriched Miklos' life, reduced the number of his seizures, and learned to "report" any problems to Miklos' parents, thus relieving them of the burden of continuous monitoring.

- And then to see how the dog training experience has changed the life of Sue. She has trained dozens of dogs destined for euthanasia that have improved the lives of people in a most remarkable way. Sue is a hero to countless people and that's certainly far above average.

- And then there's Spike and Mittens, cats that seem to have a real sense of devotion to people needing them. Spike was in very bad physical condition when he arrived at the San Francisco Society for the Prevention of Cruelty to Animals (SF/SPCA); his owners, disgusted, suggested he be euthanized. The staff at SF/SPCA cared for him and discovered he was a "hugger," that is, he hugged people in a special way. At this same time a Community Mental Health Center contacted the SF/SPCA Animal-Assisted Therapy (AAT) program about getting a "therapy" cat. Spike seemed to be the appropriate cat for people with chronic health problems or those who were overwhelmed by stress. After a suitable training period, Spike was taken to the Community Health Center. His gentle irresistible manner seemed to be made for the Center. He rejected no one and seemed to sense those who needed special attention. His presence seemed to relax patients and was a good reason for them to return for needed follow-up.

- Or to see Mittens, who was brought to a veterinary clinic for euthanasia. Instead of euthanasia, Dr. M. Doering placed Mittens on a special diet and allowed her to have a free run of the kennel room. Given tender loving care she became a beautiful, affectionate cat and was considered a good prospect for a nursing home visitation program that up to that point had used only dogs. In the nursing home there was an elderly lady in a wheelchair who was also hearing impaired. She had ignored and repulsed any offers of dogs in previous visits. On the day of Mittens' first visit, after all the dogs had been placed, Mittens was released from her travel case. She went directly to the lady in the wheelchair and jumped onto her lap. The lady smiled and immediately began to talk to Mittens about how lonely she was since she no longer had her cat, Bella, to make her smile. A nurse said that the lady had hardly said a word during her seven-month residence until Mittens came.

- To see Cashew, a golden retriever trained by Canine Companions for Independence and assigned to Melissa who was in a wheelchair. Melissa's words express better than I can her feelings about her dog:

Dear Friends:

I want to tell you about my best friend, his name is Cashew. He is a big and smart Golden Retriever and can do lots of things for me like pick up my pencils when I drop them and he brings me my dolls and he is always picking up my shoes. He turns off the lights when we leave the room to go for a walk and pulls me in my wheelchair. He is fun to go shopping with, which I could never do before. We play ball and have fun together and we love each other very much.

Melissa
(Courtesy Bonita Bergin)

I could go on for pages about what's happening in many parts of the world by modest and simple intervention of carefully selected animals. That is why I'm spending the rest of my days (and many nights) in this effort.

Another one of my "crusades" is mentioned in one of the presentations in this volume in which I describe a number of things I would do if were dictator (in "The Importance of Animals to the Well-Being of People"). I keep adding to the list. This idea is a suggestion to establish animal care facilities in certain industries and business establishments. Although I have already outlined several benefits of such a program, I feel the need to add another, and that is to provide support to people who have suffered loss of a significant other, whether person or pet. During times of great sorrow, the need to be nurtured with unconditional love is great. Animals can provide this unconditional love, and the close proximity of animals in the work place could greatly facilitate the healing process. Having lost a child (our older daughter, Karen, in Cameroon, West Africa, which was the ultimate of tragedy) as well as many animals, and having listened to many grieving people, I know how important it is to have a compassionate understanding listener or a nurturing companion, be it a person or an animal.

In closing I want to emphasize the need for a compassionate, nurturing curriculum. The experience in too many schools is to deny nurturing opportunities. There is little opportunity for a child to interact and learn and be assisted by one slightly older. There is little opportunity to interact and care for animals of various kinds from mammals to lower forms such as insects and to learn about their places in the ecosystem. Raising and tending plants from seeds is also not a norm. The importance of habitat may be shown on a video, but it is seldom experienced. (See "Recent Discoveries About Our Relationships with the Natural World" in this book.)

The reason this nurturing curriculum is so important is that many experts believe we have a limited time to save some vital areas of our planet. If we don't change some of our destructive environmental practices, it will not be fit for habitation. Everyone needs to become a nurturer, but the children are the most vital members of society in this regard as we plan and prepare for a better tomorrow.

Onward and upward! "Leaves turned to flame" can be beautiful—it's all in the eyes of the beholder.

More Than Scholars

In 1967 I was contacted by Colonel Milton Mater who was planning a National Army Research and Development Symposium at Oregon State University. He asked that I address "Projected Effects of the Humane Technology Philosophy on Research and Development in the 1970s." The assigned topic was a formidable one. For starters, Colonel Mater sent me an article by Admiral Rickover on humanistic technology. I then went to the library and spent innumerable hours there. Out of all my reading, I developed something I named (partially in jest) Bustad's Laws, which I have been extending and modifying for many audiences during the past three decades. In recent times, I felt I should change the title to Leo's Laws so that no one named Bustad would be embarrassed by them.

This talk was first presented at an Army Research and Development seminar at Oregon State University in 1968. A significant part of it (about ten laws) was presented at a Phi Kappa Phi initiation banquet in 1975 at WSU and published in the *National Forum* in 1977 (which kindly gave permission to publish in this book).

This is a time of tremendous and disturbing change for American corporations and for science and technology. The volume of products, goods and services in the Western World has changed the lives and hopes of more people more drastically than has any political upheaval in history. Political parties encouraged making the economy favorable for growth, and labor unions became eager and conservative participants in the cry for more. The communist nations wanted to emulate us. Industry said, "Find a need and fill it." Madison Avenue said, "If there is no need, create one." So we built and sold cars with the slogan, "More power than you'll ever need," and we made umbilical brushes for the Man Who Has Everything. The worldwide symbol of the past two decades became the Gross National Product, an unreliable and improper criterion in my view.

We invented and presided over a system that was probably the most productive in the use of resources ever achieved. It was a system that gave every appearance of being exportable. When we, as the generation that built industrialized America, surveyed the scene we saw different things from what our children saw. Although our children were benefiting from great and unprecedented freedom, they surveyed the scene with jaundiced eyes. We saw the successes, and they found the casualties: the hungry, the illiterate, the migrants whom we, the establishment, had conveniently screened out of our consciousness. We saw the Gross National Product, and they saw the by-products—mindless urbanization; pollution of air, land and sea; and shameful disregard of the elderly.

People had become merely numbers, unnurtured cogs in a complex machine. The era of loyalty to one's country and duties gave way in many quarters to a vast pessimism. The spring of hope had changed to a winter of despair. In reference to this, Arthur Toynbee said that the greatest challenge of our time was the morality gap between our cumulative accelerated advance in science and technology, and our appalling failure in our relations with each other.

It is well to ask how we reached this critical juncture. In a sentence or two, the problem is that we gained power and prevailed on planet Earth by developing a time-conscious, materialistic, future-oriented society with sophisticated technical skill which has fallen out of balance with the natural world about us. Change has been equated with progress. Life has been made easier, but ever more dependent on technical developments. Artificial demands have been stimulated at an ever-increasing pace, thereby devouring precious resources.

Relative to the assigned subject, I define "humane" as having a disposition to treat other human beings or animals with kindness and compassion. Humane technology would be the keeping of people and machines in balance so that we can use the machine to our betterment and not be used by the machine. At the same time, we must have reverence for all of life.

Could it be that the set of values which guide our activities as scientists, the scientific way of knowing what we are using and by which we are acting, has a basic flaw? I remind you of what the late and great J. Robert Oppenheimer (Mendelsohn, 1973) said while recalling his work on the atomic bomb: "It is my judgment in these things that when you see something that is technically sweet, you go ahead and do it and you argue about what to do about it only after you have had your technical success."

In my view, a reconstructed science would value truth, but also compassion. In the words of Everett Mendelsohn (1973), a distinguished professor at Harvard, it would "have an inbuilt ethic that would defend both being and living; that is, knowledge that would be non-violent, non-coercive, non-exploitative, non-manipulative." If that occurred, instead of having dominion over nature, we would "caress it lovingly." Then science would not be in its current sorry state relative to public acceptance.

This information provides a basis and serves to introduce the subject I wish to discuss with you—"More Than Scholars."

To Be a Scholar Is Not Enough! Other attributes are necessary. To help you understand this, I'm going to share with you some of my laws. I want to make it clear that what I'm going to say is not especially scholarly or erudite. In fact, it's rather simple. By way of explanation, I recall an event from the life of Charlie Brown, with whom I identify at this point; I am grateful to Charles Schulz, the author of *Peanuts*, for this.

Charlie and his two friends Lucy and Linus are on a small hill. Lucy comments, "Aren't the clouds beautiful? They look like big balls of cotton." Then all three lie down on their backs on the hill, looking skyward. Lucy comments further, "I could just lie here all day and watch them drift by. If you use your imagination, you can see lots of things in the cloud formations. What do you think you see, Linus?"

Linus confidently makes the following observations. "Well, those clouds up there look to me like the map of British Honduras in the Caribbean, and that cloud up there looks a little like the profile of Thomas Eakins, the famous painter and sculptor, and that group of clouds over there gives me the impression of the stoning of Stephen. I can see the apostle Paul standing there to one side."

Lucy interrupts at this point and says, "Uh, huh! That's very good, and what do you see in the clouds, Charlie Brown?"

"Well," says Charlie, "I was going to say I saw a ducky and a horsie, but I changed my mind." Unlike Charlie Brown, I haven't changed my mind. I'm going to tell you about the ducky and the horsie.

It is probably unnecessary for me to tell you that in science we use a lot of laws. Chemists and physicists use more because they're more legalistic and pietistic than we who are biologists. The most famous laws in biology are called Murphy's laws (whose source is unknown to me). Since they have general application, I'll give them to you hurriedly to put you in the proper mood for mine.

1. Nature always sides with the hidden flaw.
2. If everything seems to be going well, obviously something has been overlooked.
3. Left to themselves, things go from bad to worse.
4. Anything that can go wrong will go wrong.
5. If there is a possibility of several things going wrong, the one that will go wrong is the one that will do the most damage.

My Laws

My *First Law* states that *we have each been allotted two ears, but only one mouth and tongue, and that for a good reason.* I'll start with two quotations. First, a Native American said, "Listen or your tongue will make you deaf." Second, I turn to one of my favorite cartoon characters in *Miss Peach* (which is drawn by Mell Lazarus). The Camp Kelly Glee Club is meeting, and Miss Peach says to Arthur, "Please join the listeners' section." Thereupon Arthur is asked, "What's wrong? Can't you sing?" To this Arthur quickly replies, "We listeners are chosen for our earnestness of expression and our quietness of breathing!"

Although there were very few publications on the subject of listening before the 1950s, a study by Dr. Rankin in 1930 in Ohio impressed me very much. He made a survey of a group of workers over a considerable period and found that 70 percent of their work day was spent in communication of which 9 percent was spent in writing, 16 percent in reading, 30 percent in speaking, and 45 percent in listening. Yet as I analyzed this, I realized that much of my educational effort was spent in learning how to write and read, a little bit of it in learning to speak, but none of it in learning how to listen.

Until very recently, few courses have been taught in comprehensive listening. Several people, like Harvey Jones at Columbia and Ralph Nichols at Minnesota, became interested in this and made surveys of their classes utilizing outstanding professors giving short talks and then testing to see how much of the material was retained by the students. It was very disturbing to them to find that after the lectures there was an average retention of about 50 percent. If they waited for two weeks or two months, they found that retention averaged only about 25 percent. Similar results have been obtained in industrial surveys, helping to explain why so many businesses fail: businesses must run at 98 percent efficiency, which is difficult to attain if listening comprehension is only 25 percent. Two technicians in the same laboratory working within a similar frame of reference usually understand each other and communicate well. Going down or up the line from the laboratory director to the animal attendant or to the laboratory technician, however, results in a good deal being lost in transmission. Other aspects of this law are discussed in this volume under the title "The Art and Importance of Listening."

Since the 1950s, I've become very concerned about the subject of listening. In spite of its overwhelming importance most people have never learned how to do it and don't spend very much time at it. It's a teachable skill that few have mastered. One of the most important things you can do for others is to listen to them. People have said to me, "You really helped me out that time," but I couldn't for the life of me remember what kind of good advice I had given. Then I recalled that I hadn't given them any advice; I had listened to them.

Now we'll have a few words on talking, the subject of Leo's *Second Law. What one says should be judged on the basis of answers to three questions: Is it Kind ? Is it True? Is it Necessary?* I hasten to add that some things that may not appear to be initially kind are kind in the long run. The hardest lessons I have learned were difficult to take for the first few days after I was given them, but in retrospect I have become grateful for the constructive criticism. In administering criticism one should be diplomatic, or as diplomatic as one might possibly be under the circumstances, while placing yourself in the other person's shoes. I do believe in C.S. Lewis' philosophy that a friend is not a friend if he or she doesn't care whether I lie, cheat and steal.

We're too often breaking people with our unkind words, our innuendoes, our gossip and our untruths, by not leveling with them, and by our lack of humor. When we break people, we have what we've got—a broken world.

My *Third Law* states that *the trouble ain't that people don't know anything; the trouble is that much of what they know ain't true.* I could expound on this at great length, but to realize the truth of it, all we have to do is recall how we've performed in examinations. How many times have we thought we were right when we were wrong? Or take newspapers. How many times have we read about events that are familiar to us—but quite different from what the writer presents? Then we know we haven't come very far since 1912 when one of the most distinguished physicians in America reportedly stood before the Yale graduating class in medicine and said that he had two disturbing pieces of information for them. The first was that half of what they were taught wasn't true. The second was even more disturbing. He didn't know which half it was.

Two areas which relate to my Third Law and are of special concern to me because of their importance and impact are the news media and the legal profession. Much appears in the news today that is either slanted or just plain untrue. Some of it is downright dishonest and designed to mislead. In too many places we have an irresponsible press. However, this is not new. For example, I have never forgiven the newspapers for misreporting our invasion of Africa in 1942. The group I was with had taken Casablanca and we were chagrined to learn that the newspaper headlines in the States had read "Armored Infantry Marines Take Casablanca." The nearest armor was out of gas 15 miles out of town, and the nearest Marine was probably walking post in Spain at the embassy in Madrid.

My concern stems in part from my recognition that the press is the most powerful single influence on American opinion. This power should carry with it great obligations and responsibilities. The responsibility would be altered if we, the parents and educators, did a better job of educating both the readers and writers.

It seems that the editors, individuals and groups with nothing to say can say it very expediently by mass communication, especially if they have a knowing press agent, a reputation or an active pressure group, or if they have bad or critical information to announce. The publishers cater to and help to perpetuate people's penchant for bad news. At the same time, those with something to say have a hard time getting it said (or corrected) in the newspapers if it runs counter to the owners' and editors' prejudices or to those of opposing pressure groups. This is unfortunately true also in professional and technical publications.

A good example of this use of the press was noted by Phil Handler, President of the National Academy of Sciences, at a meeting of the Federation of American Societies of Experimental Biology. He castigated, and rightfully so, the professional biologists who, in attempting to establish national policy, kept repeating horror stories about the all-too-genuine deterioration of the environment when they could have been seeking a genuine, quantitative evaluation of the problem. The result of such recklessness is of great cost to society. What is a serious void is the ignorance of science by most citizens.

The press also has a great obligation and responsibility in influencing people's attitudes towards local, national and global issues. For example, the *New York Times* recently declared that pollution was the *cause of the year*. Important as that is, however, unfashionable human problems must still have top priority. Fighting for justice, a good education and health service for everyone and fighting against depersonalization, hunger and malnutrition must take priority over wildlife (and that said from a bird watcher). My good friend, the late Chuck Dunham of the National Academy of Sciences, said it better: "The current public panic reaction to environmental contamination threatens to cause us to lose sight of man himself in the totality of the biosphere. Right now it seems easier to get attention and votes for the environment than for man's own physical, intellectual and spiritual needs." The press has an obligation not to forget human rights even at the seeming expense of such popular issues.

As important as freedom of the press is—I say this in the full realization that our well-being is dependent on our environment—it must be a responsible freedom. One cannot really separate people, animals and environment. And there has to be room for differing views, for truth is born in enlightened controversy. By enlightened controversy, I rule out the right to lie as a deliberate instrument of policy or the right to be deliberately or irresponsibly in error. In sum, the press should be a swift reflection of our history. The expression of these historic experiences should be true, and adequate provisions should be made to detect and correct error.

Now I'll briefly address the legal profession. I fear for the future, in part, because the legal profession runs the country. In this regard I share the feelings of one of the founding fathers of this country: "I fear for America because I believe in a just God." A significant part of the legal profession seems to be more interested in applying techniques to win cases than in seeing that justice is done. There seems to be a growing disparity between judgments awarded and justice. The reason I'm gravely concerned is because the legal profession is so potentially hazardous. This is because its representatives are so logically dishonest and greed has invaded their ranks as it has in many professions, including my own. I am encouraged that many responsible attorneys are concerned about the serious problems in the legal profession and are attempting to do something about it.

Leo's *Fourth Law* states: *To believe that people act logically is illogical.* Plato realized this when he discussed misology, which he said is one of the worst things that can happen to a human being. A misologist is a person who, having become discouraged by his inability in dialectics (that is, to reason logically in an argument), concludes that careful reasoning has no value and thus shifts the blame from himself and his own ineptitude. I have a cartoon that shows a lady who sums up the plight of so many saying, "All that I know is that I stopped listening to reason and my headache was gone."

Misology plagues us now. How else can we explain the fact that in an institution devoted to learning and supported by the public for that purpose, the words of a speaker are so drowned out by the noise of the dissidents that no one hears what is being said. It does not portend well that in many quarters the importance of reason is not even understood or is just ignored. There is something called academic freedom that many people, including university professors, talk about but choose to ignore if it suits their purpose. There are too many among us who are like the desert nomad who each evening would light his lamp and feast on a bowl of dates. One evening the first two dates he picked up had worm holes in them so he laid them aside, turned off the light and then went back to the bowl and ate the rest of the dates. The light of knowledge is something he didn't want. We will do well to heed the advice of Oregon State University's President, Dr. MacVicar, who said we should substitute the University as the seat and servant of reason instead of a political agency.

My *Fifth Law* states: *Self-discipline is the price of freedom.* We hear much of freedom in the contemporary scene: "Freedom, man; that's what it's all about!" We go our merry way doing what we please. But it soon becomes obvious to the thinking person that empty freedom is really a snare and a delusion. Doing what comes naturally or easily brings only confusion, inner conflict and disaster. Without discipline of time, for example, we spoil the next day the night before. At this point, I recall T.H. Huxley's observation that a person's worst difficulties begin when he or she is able to do as he or she likes. A corollary to this is: A people and a civilization collapse when you try to give them everything they want.

As compassionate as we must be with others, we dare not be soft and indulgent with ourselves. Excellence comes at a price, and one of the major prices is inner control. We have not come very far if we have not faced the basic paradox of freedom. It is this: We are most bound when we are free, but bound in a very special way; what matters is the character of our binding (which is sort of like chemistry). The athlete who is unwilling to discipline his or her body by regular exercise and rigorous self-discipline is not free to excel on either track or field. Failure to train rigorously denies him or her the freedom to clear the bar at the desired height or to break the tape in the desired time with speed and endurance. What I have said of the athlete also applies to the scientist, to the artist, to the craftsman, to the musician, to students, to all of us. Yes, self-discipline is the price of freedom, and freedom is necessary to be creative. The true test of freedom is not so much what we are free to do, but what we are free not to do.

I add an important postscript to this law as I recall for you what the famous Alex Haley (1976) said. I should first tell you Haley is among our most capable writers and his book *Roots* is one of the most powerful dramas. Haley said that discipline is worth more than talent. It should also impress you that Haley stated in the same interview, "God is as real as the earth to me."

Roots also impressed me in another way and helped me resolve an issue in my own life. This very distressing incident in my life occurred during Christmas vacation at an international dialogue center in the Cascade Mountains of Washington state in the 1970s. As a former prisoner of war, I was asked to read "Christmas Eve in Prison" by Hanns Lilje from his book *The Valley of the Shadow* (1950). I was privileged to meet this remarkable man who was imprisoned by Hitler's Third Reich. Although I was very familiar with this book, I read Lilje's account of his Christmas eve in prison several times in hopes of stabilizing my emotional state in preparation for the reading before the assembled audience.

The reading went well, but on finishing I broke into uncontrollable sobbing and bolted from the building and went to my room; it took at least 20 minutes before I ceased sobbing. This had never happened to me and begged for an explanation. I found the answer in *Roots* in this observation by Alex Haley: "A sob hit me somewhere around my ankles; it came surging upward, and flinging my hands over my face, I was just bawling, as I hadn't since I was a baby, 'Meester Kinte.' I just felt like I was weeping for all of history's incredible atrocities against fellowmen, which seems to be mankind's greatest flaw." This answered a perplexing concern.

Related to the law on freedom and self-discipline is my corollary to my *Fifth Law. Personal emancipation is not a panacea.* Emphasis on personal emancipation has intensified in the last decade, even in the most profound intellectual circles, and has been instrumental not only in forming the values, but also in governing the lives of a generation now growing up.

However, ignorance and stupidity are often manifest in what people regard as emancipation. The problem stems from emancipation's concentration on escaping from bonds, not strengthening them. Emancipation has much more to do with power than with love, except self-love, for the object of emancipation is self, not the relationship of self to someone else. Emancipation stresses terms like self-awareness, self-determination, self-discovery, self-expression, self-fulfillment, self-identity, self-realization, self-sufficiency, and self-sustenance (but never self-abnegation).

Although it is loudly pronounced that the relationships between people will be better if the participants have been emancipated, that is not the principal goal. In reality, what unfortunately may result is only self-indulgence. No matter how good a relationship may be, if it gets in the way of self-fulfillment, it's the relationship that must go. In my opinion it is no coincidence that more people today are living alone, that more couples choose to remain childless. Fewer are getting married; more are getting divorced. Cohabitation for convenience takes the place of commitment. And in the age of emancipation when there is much talk of healthier relationships, there appear to be fewer and fewer happy marriages.

In my experience and others', there can be nothing greater in life than the happy human exchange and mutual self-fulfillment which result when people grow and mature in a life-long marriage. Certainly it is one of the great possibilities—perhaps the greatest possibility—that life has to offer. It is mysteriously beautiful, indescribably moving, often arresting and not infrequently dazzling. Its value becomes more indelibly fixed as one becomes cognizant of the finiteness of life and the inevitability of death. Nothing brings the goodness of a lasting relationship, a commitment to someone else, more into focus than that.

My *Sixth Law* states: *No one can be a whole person except by possessing compassion, reverence and intellectual integrity.* Dr. Albert Schweitzer has reminded us of these three ingredients more than most in this century. He was honored (as few men are in their lifetime) for what he really was; he was a whole person. He possessed great compassion which was manifested in his plaintive call: "We live in a dark and frightening age. This results from science and technological development of weapons with increased destructiveness. This has led to a sharp rise in inhuman actions and inhuman ideology." He asked, "When will all the killing that necessity imposes upon us be undertaken with sorrow?"

In *Out of My Life and Thought* (1953) Dr. Schweitzer also said, "A man is ethical only when life, as such, is sacred to him, that of plants and animals as that of his fellow man, and when he devotes himself helpfully to all life that is in need of help." And about humane man he wrote, "He feels the happiness in helping living things and shielding them from suffering and annihilation."

Leo's *Seventh Law* states: *Intelligence can co-exist with a want of sensibility and sensitivity.* Reverence for life is of great significance to me in my work, for I have dealt with experimental animals. My associates and I have to ask before each experiment, "Is this trip necessary?" We must also ask another question, "What will it cost if we don't perform the experiment?" I have noted that some people have little regard for life of lower forms and, therefore, I remind you of this. We must show sensibility and sensitivity to our animals, and the greatest of these is sensitivity.

The next two laws I'll give without comment. The *Eighth Law* states: *There is no complex problem which, looked at in the proper way, doesn't become more complex.* The *Ninth Law* states: *You can't tell people what they need to know because they want to know something else* (from George McDonald).

The *Tenth Law* states: *The mantle of the prophet lies uneasily on the scientist.* David Halberstam in *The Best and the Brightest* (1971) makes this point when he quotes Sam Rayburn's reaction to Vice President Lyndon Johnson's enthusiasm about the new men in the Kennedy Administration and their "map" of the future: "Well, Lyndon, you may be right and they may be every bit as intelligent as you say...but I'd feel a whole lot better about them if just one of them had run for sheriff once."

The *Eleventh Law* states: *Facts aren't everything.* Most people don't argue with facts given in evidence in this day and age, do they? Eve and Adam didn't either. In Genesis 3:6 are listed good and sufficient facts to justify getting hooked on apples from a certain tree. Recall the facts. The apples on this tree were:

- Good for food,
- a delight to the eyes, and
- able to make one wise.

With such advantages, think how many we could sell on television today. These facts give one confidence. You don't argue with facts like that, do you? Or consider these facts:

- An airplane that flies 1,500 miles an hour,
- a defoliant that defoliates everything, and
- a bug killer that kills every bug.

That is what we want, isn't it? These facts instill confidence. They make the product marketable and acceptable.

And this serves to introduce the subject of the ends and the means—with my *Twelfth Law: That nightingales sing better if you put out their eyes is not a sufficient reason to put out their eyes.* A discussion of the means and the end used to be a philosophical discussion. Now it is expressed in terms of technical facts on the basis of which one makes a practical decision. Today it seems everything has become means. We have lost our way or, perhaps more correctly, we don't know where we are going. We ignore the end, and we have concentrated on the means. We set huge machines in motion in order to arrive nowhere. That doesn't say we don't have some ends—to succeed in competition, to get a higher salary, to get a newer car or a bigger house—but these ends are not valid.

People must be total producers, and they must be obedient consumers, ingesting everything that economics puts in their mouths (i.e., tells them on television). While trying to obtain happiness for people, we are turning them into instruments of the modern gods—means. These modern gods are no better than the new batches of gods shipped in from the East to Olympus in Caesar's day when the old gods of Rome were dying. For these gods were no better than the old ones; a whole pantheon of modern gods are worthless if they have nothing to say to the person with a broken heart. What really happens in this technological age is that people become means, and it happens so logically. In order to make people happy we must give them plenty of goods to consume. To achieve this, production must be organized and then consumption adapted to production.

Few people are moved to ask where we are going or to check the direction we are moving. The ends seem to have disappeared. Means seem to create more means. New kinds of production appear because new machines have been created—or we have discovered new ways of exploiting matter. It is of little or no consequence that we may not need these new products or that these new products are really useless—like umbilical brushes for the Man Who Has Everything. We rejoice whenever a new speed record is realized and work hard to go even faster, often killing people in the process as if speed were a valid end in itself. But thereby we save so much time—for what?

We do the same in the healing arts to extend the work of healing. Some of my associates and I have worked long days and not a few nights and weekends on the elusive causes of cancer—on means for early diagnosis or control to save lives. But why? In too many places today time and life no longer have meaning. People don't seem to know what to do with their time. Proof enough of this is the hours spent by millions in front of the idiot box drinking beer, eating popcorn, growing bigger and bigger waffle butts and smaller and smaller minds. Life has become more absurd than ever. Why? Because the spiritual foundations of time and of life have been destroyed in the hearts of people. The autocracy of means has also invaded the spiritual sphere. People today have been dehumanized by means, so life and time are of no real significance. If one would examine this situation carefully, probably he or she would find that no civilization has been so wasteful of the time and lives of human beings as ours.

The means now justify the means, for in our day everything that succeeds, everything that is effective, everything that is efficient is justified. The measuring criteria are quicker, greater or more precise; we are surrounded by marvelous successes while people starve. When practices become commonplace, people accept them. The Russian Communist did not shudder over the camps in Siberia; the Nazis in Germany, in fact many Germans I saw in 1944 and 1945 as a prisoner of war, did not react with horror to the presence of extermination camps. Alexander Pope (1843) described this process in *An Essay on Man*:

> Vice is a monster of so frightful mien,
> As to be hated needs but to be seen;
> Yet seen too oft, familiar with her face
> We first endure, then pity, then embrace.

We have become immune to catastrophic dimensions. People being killed—yes, even mass genocide—doesn't seem to shake us any more.

At this point, I recall for you an experiment described by an acquaintance of mine, Jerome Frank, in his book *Sanity and Survival* (1968). It has been described on television. I believe it has something to say about humaneness and humane technology. As stated in his book, "The subjects—normal American college students and adults—believed that the purpose of the experiment was to study the effect of punishment on learning. Each subject was to present a fellow subject (actually an experimenter's accomplice) with a simple learning task and shock him each time he made a mistake." Frank explained that the experiment was set up in such a way that all subjects truly believed they were administering volts of shock. As accomplices made errors, the subjects increased the voltage. The voltage administered finally reached a level where the accomplice pounded the wall and, then, stopped signaling answers. The subject was told to regard this as an error and to increase the voltage again. When the subject hesitated, Frank said that the order was given, "You have no choice, you must go on."

This experiment resulted in very disturbing findings. "All subjects administered shocks up to 300 (painful shock), and 62 percent went to the maximum—

450 volts (two levels beyond 'danger, severe shock')." Certainly this gives us some real cause for deep concern as we contemplate the future.

People in many quarters no longer seek to know themselves in order that they may acquire self-mastery. As a result they are used not by God but by a system or a machine. This brings me to *Law Thirteen: One cannot live effectively without a meaning for his or her life.* The why of life is infinitely more important than the how of life. Many people are motivated or dominated by a will-to-pleasure, not a few by a will-to-power. But aware persons are dominated by a longing and a striving to find the meaning of life—the ultimate meaning of life itself. They are dominated by a will-to-meaning. Nietzsche understood this when he said, "If we have our own *why* of life, we shall get along with almost any *how.*" Albert Camus addressed this, too, in *Caligula* when Cherea states, "To lose one's life is no great matter; when the time comes I'll have the courage to lose mine. But what's intolerable is to see one's life being drained of meaning, to be told there's no reason for existing. A man can't live without some reason for living." In an address at Concordia College, Al Rogness made this point so well in his discussion of the ultimate question, "Why live?"

"What do you do?" he asked the farmer.

"I raise pigs."

"Why?"

"So people can eat."

"Why should they eat?"

"So they can live."

"Why should they live?"

"So they can raise more pigs."

The tragedy of it all is that this is the story of too many lives.

And this brings me to the *Fourteenth Law: You shall love!* It's what the Danish philosopher Kierkegaard called the Royal Law. The poet Auden was even more definite; he stated we must learn to love or die. And we need this. In *Mother Night* (1961), Kurt Vonnegut's Campbell said, "No matter what I was really, no matter what I really meant, uncritical love was what I needed and my Helga was the angel who gave it to me—copiously. No young person on earth is so excellent in all respects as to need no uncritical love!" This love at work in a person or a community transforms. It knows intellectual charity, vulnerability, peace, joy. With it one learns to live with few defenses and with one's deficiencies—without being judgmental. There is a naturalness, a healing quality and a wholesomeness about it that one would give anything to share. To see it at work is to know that's how it ought to be.

Vannevar Bush (1967), a great scientist and scholar, had something to say about this: "The process of evolution did not teach us to rejoice in the beauty of nature. Nor did it produce the concepts of honor and integrity. The making of a poem or the benediction of music in an open field at dusk has little to do with crass survival, yet here they are. Love can reach far higher than the needs of propagation demand. It can produce new life, but it can also make life worth living."

My next quotation is from *The Little Prince* (1943). Antoine de Saint Exupery captured a great truth in simple words: "'And now here is my secret', said the fox to the Little Prince, 'A very simple secret: It is only with the heart that one can see rightly; what is essential is invisible to the eye.'"

I cannot close without a word of caution. The road ahead is difficult. Success will be a long hard pull. We must build bridges instead of barriers, or we will learn too late the truth of Leo's Corollary to Nero's Number One Law. Nero's Law was "Burn, Baby, Burn!" My corollary to this is: "It took many years to build Rome, but only a few days to burn it." Whether it is biological evolution or social evolution, constant vigilance is necessary to prevent discarding the essential with the trivial and the significant with the inconsequential. We must be patient in making important decisions; we must realize every change is not an improvement; few violent revolutions have improved the lot of people.

We must realize that we live in an imperfect world, but that we are here to make it better. If we cannot do anything else, we should at least work at treating one another as human beings made in the image of God and respect what Albert Schweitzer (1923) said about reverence: "But the ethic of reverence for life constrains all...to give themselves as men to the man who needs human help and sympathy. It does not allow the scholar to live for his science alone, even if he is very useful to the community in doing so....It demands from all that they should sacrifice a portion of their own lives for others."

The Art And Importance Of Listening

*In the late 1940s and early 1950s, I became very concerned about the inability of most peo-
ple to listen effectively and all the problems that resulted from this deficiency. On the other
hand, I was impressed with the attractiveness and helpfulness of people who were effective,
compassionate listeners. The lack of information on listening distressed me. I discussed this
void with a dear friend, Dr. Ken Erickson, an educator and superintendent of schools in
Corvallis, Oregon (later a professor at the University of Oregon). He provided information
about Professor Ralph Nichols' work on listening at the University of Minnesota (Nichols
and Steven, 1957), and from his work I learned about the studies of Dr. H.E. Jones at
Columbia University in 1923 and Dr. P.T. Rankin, Ohio State University, in 1930. But
they were lonely voices.*

*Listening, I have learned, is hard and very demanding work. I had this indelibly
imprinted on me after my wife lost her hearing, obtained hearing aids and learned lip reading. She is exhausted after 15 to 20 minutes of concentrated listening. I am convinced that
the lives of countless people would be greatly enhanced and enriched, students would learn
and retain much more information, and businesses and professions would be far more efficient and effective if they learned how to listen. That is why I've given this talk countless
times to a variety of groups and to the incoming professional students when I was dean.*

The frequent lament of every parent, every child, every husband,
every wife, every teacher, every student is this: You have ears, but you do
not hear. God and the prophets had some problems with this, too. In fact, if
you're one of those who count references in the Bible, you'll find out that the
number of references to hearing and listening in the Bible number about 1,200,
which is probably greater than any other subject. So, I assume that this is an
important subject. And to me, it is. I could now spend the rest of my allotted
time giving you examples of poor listening, but I'm not going to do that. I'll tell
only one. Lars hadn't been feeling well, and as far as he could recall, he had
never had a physical exam in his 67 years. So he made an appointment with a
local practitioner in my hometown. When he arrived at the doctor's office, the
receptionist-nurse ordered him to strip to the waist, so Lars took off his pants. I
consider that poor listening!

I became interested in this subject when I realized that many people, myself
included, were poor listeners. I was deeply disturbed when I would give tests to

students on material on which I had lectured so "masterfully"—and they weren't able to come up with the right answers! Nevertheless, I do feel qualified to talk on listening because I have been married for so long and also have been a dean.

I came to realize that the ability to listen was a teachable skill that few had mastered. The inability to listen contributed to failures in all aspects of every life. I'll never forget my first meeting with the world famous writer and psychiatrist, Dr. Paul Tournier, in Geneva, Switzerland. I asked, "What do you tell people who have lost a child or have one who is critically ill?" And I recalled the tragedies that had befallen some people I had known in the recent past. "What do you tell the father and mother of the 27-month-old child—their firstborn son—who drowns in the neighbor's pool? And what should I have told a friend of a good friend of mine here in Geneva when his daughter Karen, ten years old, had manifested some swelling in the throat, and it was diagnosed as lymphoma? What do you tell these people?" My question probably sounded desperate to Paul Tournier, and it was. After considerable hesitation he said, "I do a lot of listening."

I have heard that 98 percent of what we learn, we learn through our eyes and our ears. My wife once said, "If I had to lose either my hearing or my sight, I would rather lose my sight." When she first said this I was quite shocked. After studying the subject and doing considerable thinking about it, I have more sympathy for her point of view. Loss of sight can separate one from things; loss of hearing can separate one from people.

Midway through this century, there was a flurry of activity on listening as an important communication skill and I learned of an early survey made by Dr. Rankin (1930) at Ohio State University. He did what we did at General Electric Company in the 1950s. We kept an inventory of how we spent each day. Rankin found that 70 percent of the day of his surveyed group was spent in communication. (For the student it is probably higher.) He found that the group they studied spent 9 percent of their communication time writing, 16 percent reading, 30 percent speaking, and 45 percent listening. (Leo's *First Law* states that we have two ears and one mouth—and probably for a very good reason.)

The time we've spent learning to communicate bears no relationship to the time these people spend in the various areas of communicating with others. Your experience is probably like mine. You spent 12 to 16 years learning how to read and write and probably took a course or two in public speaking; but as for learning about listening comprehension, we just haven't had the course. I guess we're supposed to learn this by osmosis! In the 1950s, you probably would have found only Stevens College (a women's college) teaching a course in listening—as one of the social graces. In the early 1950s, if you had looked up 3,000 articles on communication, you would have found very few on listening. But there is, fortunately, a growing body of information on listening and more courses are being offered on listening. Honeywell Corporation was teaching a course on listening in the 1960s. They obtained it from Basic Systems in New York who developed a curriculum based mainly on material from Prof. Ralph G. Nichols of the University of Minnesota (personal communication, William J. Durnberger, 1967).

It should be very disturbing to every professional to deliver a well-prepared lecture and then find that his or her students only retained about 50 percent of it, if they were tested right away. There have been studies to verify this. It should be even more disturbing that had the students been tested two weeks or two months after the lecture rather than immediately, the retention figure would have been only 25 percent (Jones, 1923; Bormann et al., 1969). This is true also in industry, especially if you go from the general manager to the person on the assembly line. There is a tremendous amount lost in such an interchange. Many businesses fail and poor listening comprehension is at least partially to blame. Many marriages and friendships fail for this reason, too.

Characteristics of a Bad Listener

One of the many contributions of Professor Nichols is that he prepared a list of the characteristics of a bad listener. I have modified and added to his list. As I give them to you, I'm certain you'll recognize many of them in your friends, and perhaps in the cool of tomorrow morning you'll even recognize some of them in yourselves.

The first thing the poor listener does is decide that the subject is uninteresting and useless, and that the speaker doesn't deserve a hearing, so the listener "turns the speaker off."

You're going to be trapped many times as you are trapped here today, but accept it as a challenge. What is in it for me? G.K. Chesterton was a famous English writer; he's a favorite of mine, not only because he wrote beautiful prose and poetry, but because he also wrote some very beautiful things about pigs. He observed that there is no such thing as an uninteresting subject—just uninterested listeners. So, the take-home lesson is that even if the announced subject is "The Care of Camellias in Nuclear Attack," you want to concentrate and see if maybe you couldn't get something out of it that would be helpful.

The second characteristic of a bad listener is that he or she waits to deliver a speech carefully rehearsed while listening. You really can't do it that way.

And the third one is something like the second; the bad listener listens carefully for flaws in the presentation so that at the first opportunity he or she can clobber the speaker. That really isn't good listening either.

The fourth characteristic of a bad listener is that he or she fails to comprehend nonverbal communication. I'm really "one leg up" on most of you in this regard. I've spent much of my life learning nonverbal communication because we veterinarians have to diagnose abnormal or normal conditions in animals, and they can't always tell us "where it hurts." Our patients, however, don't lie to us; so that's a mixed blessing. With experience, I have learned to understand nonverbal communication in people. And I can pretty much tell where the people are coming from when they come to the office in the morning, but I don't want you to tell them that.

It's also very important—and I learned this early—that we must respect the physiology of the other person in our nonverbal communication. I learned this with my wife shortly after we were married. I'm a "Type A" guy; I get up early and cook my own breakfast. I realized that getting my wife up to cook me a breakfast at 5:30 in the morning was asking her to do something that she was incapable of doing. She would get up, find her way to the kitchen, turn on the right rear burner, and put the tea kettle on the front left. She'd put raisins in my Russian tea and generally jazz things up. I mean, it was a disaster. I realized that we weren't destined for a long marriage this way, so I made a deal with my wife. She'd stay in bed until I would leave for work which was usually about 6:30 a.m. I really don't know what time she got out of bed in the morning, but she always had dinner ready for me when I came home at 6:30 in the evening. (When she lost her hearing, I found out when she got up in the morning because we trained her hearing dog to awaken her when her alarm clock went off at 6:30 a.m.)

In regard to nonverbal communication, I recall another story out of New Mexico. There was a fellow from Manhattan who went there to attend college; his roommate most of the time was a Native American from New Mexico. This fellow from Manhattan was always after his roommate to come visit New York. After each year he would say, "Now this summer, you've got to come and visit and see how the people live (or exist) in Manhattan." Well, his roommate was not able to get back east until a few years after he graduated. After his arrival, his Manhattan friend showed him all of the sights. One day when they were walking along Theater Row they came upon some potted plants on the sidewalk. The Native American said, "I hear a cricket." Well, the taxis and other cars were going up and down honking—it's really a noisy place. His friend from Manhattan said, "You're out of your tree. You can't hear a cricket here." "Oh," he says, "I'm pretty sure I do." And he walked over to one of those plants and he pulled out a cricket and he said, "There it is. You know, it all depends on what you're trained to hear." Whereupon he pulled a 50-cent piece out of his pocket, threw it down on the pavement, and ten people made a dive for it.

So, it all depends on what we're trained to hear and see. I read some statistics the other day relative to communication: 55 percent of it was body language, 38 percent of it was tone of voice, and only 7 percent were words. These were shocking observations for me to learn and I suppose also for anyone who spends much of life lecturing and choosing one's words carefully. In communication, sincerity must be manifest in our whole being.

The fifth characteristic of a bad listener is to become overly concerned with facts and details. The medical professions and others get so obsessed with this. Many of my associates in the health sciences field give percentages to four or five significant figures. For example, in a test of a new drug, seven patients out of 11 showed a beneficial response. Too often it comes out as 63.64 percent positive response instead of 64 percent or about two-thirds. I remind my associates or students who are overly concerned about insignificant details that the most important biological number is a woman's age, and it isn't significant beyond two figures. Do you really care if a woman is 39 or 39.2? And I note many of you have already reached that age. I've been 39 for a long time.

The sixth characteristic of the bad listener is that he or she can't cope with periods of silence or use them effectively. I've run an experiment on this. I'm often asked to speak before audiences like service clubs at noon. And they have a real cut-off; everybody gets up and leaves at 1:30 or, in some places, 1:00. So in order to cover the subject, I speak very rapidly. In fact, sometimes I go at about 200 words a minute, and you find out that if you speak about 200 words a minute, people will listen very carefully because they're afraid they'll miss something. And it's good for a little while. Then I stop abruptly in one of these lectures before a very large audience, and I start fumbling with my notes (which is very easy because I've had so much experience losing my place). I've observed that the natives become very restless; they start rubbing their hands together. I timed them on this; after 20-30 seconds they manifest great anxiety. They're wondering if the old geezer has had a heart attack or something.

Well, the take-home lesson here is that there are often useful periods of time during a lecture that you can use effectively. Many people that you will listen to, for example, in 50-minute lectures (which usually go on for 55 minutes) speak very slowly, at about 100 words a minute, and they often tell you some tired old stories like the ones with which I started off this lecture. And some of them give you what I call a cross between an abalone and a crocodile, which is a "crock of baloney." You should, however, learn to utilize these periods effectively to recapitulate points in the lecture. This advice comes from my 14 years of university work during which I strove diligently to find a short-cut to learning. I didn't find one outside of repetition—to use and reuse the information heard. You recapitulate these points so that at the end of the lecture you have gone over many of them several times; you're "taping" them in your mind's eye. In this way, periods of silence can be used effectively for your own enlightenment.

The seventh thing that a bad listener does is to fake attention. Now, I think you folks are all listening, but I've spoken to some audiences in which some members are like race horses at the starting gate in that they want to impress you that they're really listening. We do play games; in fact, I do it myself. After a long day at the office listening to all the troubles that people have, or at least think they have, I come home after 12 hours or so, and the Chief, my wife, wants to tell me something. However, there's this fellow on the tube—the fellow that wears a sweater now, who took Cronkite's place—Dan Rather, and there's the paper that came after I left in the morning with its headlines "staring" at me. I'm trying to listen to the Chief, but I'm really checking on Dan Rather on the tube and I'm looking at the *Spokesman-Review*. That's faking attention and it's wrong.

Now, faking attention is also quite closely related to trying to be someone you're not. When you're trying to be somebody you're not or doing something that's out of character, you're really carrying a facade. In our high school, we had a drama teacher. She was always putting on a play. And when I heard she was going to put on a play, I would try to avoid her. But we had very few students in our school so I usually ended up playing a part that I was not; that's the toughest job in the world—trying to be someone you're not.

I often tell a story about a psychiatrist at this point. In fact, I have several psychiatrist stories, but one of them I think is particularly apropos here because it has to do with faking it. This psychiatrist lived in a large town; he was also a circus buff. One day, it was past 5:00 p.m. and he had had a rough day. His receptionist knew he was about to leave, but she had a very distraught person on her hands. I mean he was lower than a snake in a wagon track. And she wasn't about to let him go without seeing the psychiatrist, so she ran into his office, caught him just as he was going out the back door, and said, "There's a person out here that you've got to listen to!" So, he heard him out. I won't give the diagnosis, but it was a sad case. And the psychiatrist was pressed, as we in the health sciences are often pressed, not only for diagnosis, but for treatment. How do you tide this fellow over for tonight? The psychiatrist had a bright idea. He confidently said, "Here's what I want you to do tonight. There's a great circus in town—a lot of great acts. I want you to take in a lot of these acts, but you won't be able to take them all in. There's one I don't want you to miss, and that's the clown." After a long period of silence his patient said, "I am that clown!" A heavy piece of merchandise to carry is a facade. Be yourself; don't fake it.

The eighth thing a bad listener does is to tolerate the bad performance of the speaker. Now that doesn't mean that before my lecture here is finished, you stand up and point out all the deficiencies of my presentation. Or next Sunday, or next Saturday, or whenever you go to church, that you stand up in the middle of the sermon (or homily) and straighten out the pastor, father, rabbi, or whoever it might be. We do owe each other the benefit of constructive criticism, but we should do it with "warm fuzzies."

If we really love somebody, we should care enough to do something about it. And it is well that you remember Leo's *Second Law* (see "More Than Scholars"): "Is it kind?" "Is it true?" "Is it necessary?" Constructive criticism will certainly shorten a lot of conversations. But as C.S. Lewis said, "Think tough, but love tenderly."

The ninth thing that a bad listener does is to shun technical and painstaking listening. While evaluating this particular characteristic, Nichols asked poor listeners what television programs they watched. From my own experiences I can mention a few programs that I would say were in the questionable category—the Democratic National Convention, the Republican National Convention, and I guess I should also say "Hogan's Heroes" because I was in prison camp, and it was nothing like that. But they were programs that you really didn't have to make the fifth grade to understand; maybe the fourth grade, but not the fifth. You can't learn comprehensive listening by listening to or watching something that you really don't have to pay much attention to. To learn comprehensive listening, you've got to really work at it.

The tenth thing that bad listeners do is to allow emotional words to throw them. Now, I don't know what your hang-ups are, but I could probably list 15 "emotional" words and I would lose all of you. You would be gone because those words direct your thoughts elsewhere. I'll give you an example from my own life. If you said Christopher Columbus discovered America, you've lost me as a listener. I had to put up with this misinformation most of my life: we, instead, had a picture on our wall at home of Leif Ericson discovering America. You see, Christopher Columbus was a "Johnny-come-lately." My forefathers were here on this continent 500 years before him. And so this is very hard for me; they're emotional words. (I send out Leif Ericson cards on Columbus Day.) So fight the feeling. Don't let emotional words throw you like they throw me.

The eleventh characteristic of a bad listener is the failure to realize that every person is unique. One of the biggest mistakes we make is to say he or she is "just an average person." If there is an average person, there is only one. They're all different, and to the extent that we recognize that, we recognize everyone we meet is a unique creation of a great Creator. Don't ever forget that. In 1941 C.S. Lewis had something to say about this. Walter Hooper (1982) reports it in *Through Joy and Beyond*:

> It is a serious thing to live in a society of possible gods and goddesses, to remember that the dullest and most uninteresting person you talk to may one day be a creature which, if you saw it now, you would be strongly tempted to worship, or else a horror and a corruption such as you now meet, if at all, only in a nightmare. All day long we are, in some degree, helping each other to one or the other of these destinations. It is in the light of these overwhelming possibilities, it is with the awe and the circumspection proper to them, that we should conduct all our dealings with one another, all friendships, all loves, all play, all politics. There are no ordinary people. You have never talked to a mere mortal. Nations, cultures, arts, civilizations—these are mortal, and their life is to ours as the life of a gnat. But it is immortals whom we joke with, work with, marry, snub and exploit—immortal horrors or everlasting splendors.

Yes, everyone is a unique person!

The twelfth thing that the bad listener does is to question for victory rather than clarification. We play those games, don't we? The professors play it with the students; the students certainly play it with the professors. At least some of the students I have in my classes do it. They're playing games with me. It's a one-upmanship kind of thing. Husbands do it to wives; wives do it to husbands. I can give you many more examples of this, where relationships, both professional and private, are jeopardized because people fall into the trap of questioning for victory, rather than questioning for clarification. I'm sure you can think of many examples, too.

The last thing that I'm going to mention to you is the thirteenth characteristic of the bad listener which appears when he or she criticizes the speaker for ineptness, for appearance, or whatever it might be. Now, I happen to have learned another language before I learned the one I'm trying to speak tonight and people sometimes recognize it. But I'm here to tell you that if somebody came running in that door right now and said, "Get outa dis rat's nest; it's on fire!" I wouldn't say, "Couch that in better rhetoric." I would get out of here! I would do what he or she said even though it was said in a crude but clear and concise language.

Most of you here tonight know me, but if I go before a strange audience they usually do a double-take on me. And they look at my clothes—something that might be on sale at the local St. Vincent De Paul or Goodwill stores. I'm wearing an unusual tie, a very special tie. Actually I think that ordinary ties are a waste of money. They're non-utilitarian—they cost money, and they collect gravy and spilled soup. And unless you're going to be a slob, you've got to get them cleaned, and that's very expensive. So I had my wife construct this tie. It's a very large, wide tie. They're called belly warmers. It's utilitarian. It's got a zipper in it. You can carry notes in it (which I'll bring to your attention in a few minutes). And you see, it's big enough so if you're going to speak to the Weight Watchers Club for lunch you can carry a sandwich in it. And a lot of places now don't serve dessert, so I carry dessert in it, too. And also, if you adjust it right, you can let it catch the soup and the gravy in the pouch and then you can zip it up, thereby saving on cleaning bills. And another thing about it is that if you wear this to a cocktail party, I can assure you before the night is out that somebody will come up to you, put his arm around you and say, "Hey, buddy. The fly on your tie is half open."

Now why do I go through all of these shenanigans? There's a very good reason for them. You didn't come here tonight to look at what I'm wearing, to make judgments on how I speak, whether I have an accent and what kind of accent it is, or my appearance. You waste your time if you say, "I would like to have that nose full of nickels," or "No wonder he's speaking about listening—his ears are so big." You came here for only one good reason and that was to see if what I had to say to you was going to help you, to be edifying, or cause you to laugh (which is the best therapy today). That's why you go to hear someone speak.

Now there is another dimension to all this. On this card in the pouch here in my tie, (my belly warmer), it says, "Keep silent or your tongue will make you deaf." That's a Native American proverb. It's a pretty good one. This other note relates to the theological dimension of listening—from Dietrich Bonhoeffer (1964), one of the great theologians of this century. He was a pacifist. However, he was involved in the attempt on Hitler's life, or accused of that, and he was taken out and shot a few weeks before I finally gained my freedom (in another prison camp). He said that the most important duty that you have to your brother and your sister in the fellowship (and this is your brother and sister in the universal sense) is to listen to them.

I have three readings for you now, and then I'll close. Richard Bach (1981) wrote that, "It's not the crowds that wear me. It's the kind of crowd that doesn't care at all about what I came to say. You can walk New York to London on the ocean. You can pull gold coins out of forever, and still not make them care you know." And when he said that, he looked lonelier than I have ever seen a man still alive. He didn't need food or shelter or money or fame. He was dying of his need to say what he knew, and nobody cared enough to listen.

The second reading is by John Godfrey. His parents were immigrants, as my parents were, and although he wanted to be something else, they said, "Lawyers run the country. You should become a lawyer." So he became a lawyer. And he set up practice in a town, purchased some land, and with time the town grew around him. When he got to be 70 or 75 years old (his wife had died), he decided he should do something for this town. So he contracted with the best architect he could find, and he built a very beautiful building. He wouldn't tell anybody what he was up to until the day of the dedication. On that day there was a sign that went over the door of this building that said, "The man who listens."

By way of explanation he said, "One of the most terrible aspects of this world today is nobody listens to anyone else. If you are sick or even dying, nobody listens. If you are bewildered or frightened or lost or bereaved or alone or lonely, nobody really listens. Even the clergy are hurried and harassed. They do their best and work endlessly, but time has taken on a fragmented character. It doesn't seem to have any substance any longer. Nobody has time to listen to anyone, not even those who love you and would die for you. Your children, your parents, your friends—they have no time. That's a very terrible thing, isn't it? Whose fault is it? I don't know, but there just doesn't seem to be any time." Now these are really the words of Taylor Caldwell (1960) in her novel *The Listener*. But you don't have to go to fiction to hear this kind of word. You can go to real life, and I give it to you from *Creative Brooding* by Robert A. Raines (1966). It's called "Too Busy to Listen:"

Dear Folks,

Thank you for everything, but I'm going to Chicago to try to start some kind of a new life. You asked me why I did those things, and why I gave you so much trouble. And the answer is easy for me to give you, but I'm wondering if you will understand. Remember when I was about six or seven, and I used to want you to just listen to me. I remember all the nice things you gave me for Christmas and my birthday. And I was really happy with the thing about a week at the time you gave me the things, but the rest of the time, and during the year, I really didn't want presents. I just wanted all the time for you to listen to me, like I was somebody who felt things too, because I remember even when I was young, I felt things. But you said you were so busy.

Mom, you're a wonderful cook, and you'd have everything so clean, and you were tired so much from doing all those things, it made you so busy. But you know something, Mom. I would have liked crackers and peanut butter just as well, if you'd have only sat down with me for awhile during the day and said to me, "Tell me all about it, so that maybe I can help you understand."

And when Donna came, I couldn't understand why everybody made so much fuss, because I didn't think it was my fault that her hair is curly and her skin's so white. And she doesn't have to wear glasses with those thick lenses either. Her grades were better, too, weren't they? Now if Donna ever has any children, I hope you will tell her just to pay some attention to the one who doesn't smile very much, because that one will really be crying inside. And when she's about to bake six or seven dozen cookies, to make sure first, that the kids don't want to tell her about a dream or a hope or something. Because thoughts are important, too, to small kids, even though they don't have so many words to use when they tell you about what's inside of them.

I think that all the kids who are doing so many of the things that grown-ups are tearing out their hair worrying about are really looking for somebody that will have time to listen a few minutes, and who really and truly will treat them as they would a grown-up, who might be useful to them or polite to them.
Love to all,

Your Son

And this was by a boy with a record of juvenile delinquency. I make no comment about it except to say that listening to someone gives them a feeling of self-worth, which is a very important commodity at this time in our society—as it is at any time.

And now my final reading. A great human being and famous columnist, Erma Bombeck (1978), recalled an important incident in her life regarding the importance of listening. Erma recounted spending a frustrating morning that was punctuated by numerous interruptions while getting ready to go to the airport. She arrived there sooner than she had hoped and rejoiced at having thirty minutes to herself to think and read before the plane took off. As she began reading, a voice next to her said, "I'll bet it's cold in Chicago." Erma tried to ignore her but she persisted in telling about her son who lived in Chicago. Then the woman said, "My husband's body is on this plane. We've been married for fifty-three years. I don't drive, you know, and when he died a nun drove me from the hospital. We aren't even Catholic. The funeral director let me come to the airport with him."

Erma recalled that she detested herself at that moment because another person was screaming to be heard by a stranger and she was more interested in a novel. Erma continued, "All she needed was a listener—no advice, wisdom, experience, money, assistance, expertise or even compassion—but just a minute or two to listen.

"She talked numbly and steadily until we boarded the plane, and then found her seat in another section. As I hung up my coat, I heard her plaintive voice say to her seat companion, 'I'll bet it's cold in Chicago.'

"I prayed, 'Please, God, let her listen.'"

We must do more than hear; we must listen with our whole being.

Freedom And Responsibility

Freedom is a popular subject, especially among those who have lost theirs or never had it. Responsibility is an unpopular concept. Most people want the privileges of a democracy as well as power in whatever society they're in, but they shy away from responsibility. Ever since my internment as a prisoner of war, the subject of freedom is seldom out of mind. For years I have collected information on it.

Shortly after I came to WSU as dean, I was asked by the members of the Military Science Department to address the ROTC members at their commissioning ceremonies. In the first talk I addressed the subject of freedom and honor, and it was published in WSU's alumni publication Hilltopics. I've presented variations of the talk in many forums and incorporated it into talks at graduations and Veterans' Day ceremonies. I presented it in abbreviated form in my hometown on the 4th of July, 1990. It's a subject that will always be in my mind and often on my lips. Freedom seems easier to lose than to win back.

My assignment today is a very difficult one for me. When my wife read the first draft of this presentation, she wiped the tears from her eyes. She asked me when I prepared it. I told her I had been preparing it for several years. I didn't have the heart to tell her it's been over 30 years in preparation. Before I begin the main text I will attempt to explain the tears. I can only guess why my wife shed tears. One reason may have been the day in 1944 when, after she received a telegram notifying her I was missing in action, she chanced to meet a soldier who had just returned from Italy. He was wearing the same army division patch as mine. She asked him if he knew Leo Bustad. He said, yes, he certainly did, for he was in my unit. He then went on to tell her that I had been killed at Anzio!

To those of you who are being honored today, I remind you it was just 35 years ago that I sat where you sit. But I was more fortunate than you; the governor of the state gave the address. He also commissioned many of us as second lieutenants and gave us orders to report to Fort Wright the next day. As we sat there that day, we all felt an uneasiness about the uncertain future of our nation. As I stand before you today I have the same uneasiness, for I am very deeply concerned about our country's future for many reasons. One of them is that in the recent past, American constitutional democracy was placed in great peril. Questions have been raised relative

Abbreviated text of an address at the ROTC Commissioning Ceremonies, Washington State University, Pullman, Washington, June 5, 1976.

to whether it will, in fact, survive even this decade. Recent conditions made our time one in which perhaps the most serious threat to liberty in American history could take place. I am here today to awaken you to the realization that our democracy is a very fragile thing indeed. Without concern and nurture and continuing vigilance, we stand to lose it. You who are being commissioned today have a special responsibility in this regard. With this brief introduction as a background, I wish to share with you some thoughts on freedom and responsibility.

On the 4th of July, 1944, I stood at attention on a dirt field inside a barbed wire enclosure in a heavily guarded compound 90 miles south of Danzig in the Polish Corridor. It was a German prison camp. I was standing at attention because our prisoner of war camp band was playing "The Star-Spangled Banner." For some strange reason, the Germans had given us permission to do this. I cannot yet understand why they allowed us to play the national anthem on our Independence Day celebration as prisoners of war. It was a day and an hour that I shall never forget, nor will any of those who were there. As a song of victory, of home, of freedom (most especially freedom), it brought chills to my whole being, tears to my eyes. Since that time I have never listened to our national anthem but that a chill goes through me. I will not say that it is difficult for me to discuss this without emotion; it is impossible. The basis for the emotion is very complex, but I want to try to analyze it for you in the next few minutes.

I know the basis is not only that day almost 32 years ago. Many other things contribute. It involved learning about freedom the hard way—by losing it. It involved, too, recalling the many sacrifices that make each day for us what it should be—a day to celebrate our freedom. In recalling my comrades who fought and fell in combat, it all goes back to almost 200 years ago when some courageous, God-fearing men subscribed to a document, a declaration that we don't, I fear, appreciate enough. Let me recall for you the last lines of the Declaration, lines that I keep in my pocket diary and refer to periodically: "And for the support of this Declaration, with a firm reliance on the protection of divine Providence, we mutually pledge to each other our Lives, our Fortunes, and our sacred Honor." The signatories were so serious about this Declaration that they signed a death warrant. They pledged everything they had, including their lives. And that's what it has cost many down through the years.

But the many who gave their lives didn't just die so that we might live, for just to live is not enough. Their lives are much too precious and much too great a price to pay just so that we might eat, drink, be merry and grow fat. It makes little sense to me that we ask the young to give their lives so that old people might grow rich. If this is all it meant, many a father and a mother and a widow would choke back bitter tears. They hoped that the loss of a loved one meant more righteousness and freedom for all of us in this country and in the world. And they have a right to that hope. They have a right to see our nation use its freedom of speech to raise its voice against all injustice and greed. They have a right to expect us to use our freedom of assembly for the purpose of a united defense of all that is true and honorable. And they have a right, also, to expect that we use our freedom of the press to publish only in accordance with the highest ethical standards for the proper welfare of humankind.

These people who have made great sacrifices have a right to such expectations, but in all candor we must admit their expectations have not been realized. With shame we must confess that for millions of Americans, freedom means simply the opportunity to do what they please. That sort of freedom is not worth one life on Casablanca, Salerno, Anzio, Normandy, Bataan, or any other field of battle that you care to name.

Some current attitudes on freedom are frightening to me. I believe that reproof and correction should come from those who really love America, not from those who would capitalize on her freedom or steal it away, or who just want to use its privileges but never take any of its responsibilities. I say this at a time when we are receiving lectures on principles from men who lack them. Incredible as it may seem, we are all being asked to logically prove that a free citizenry is a good thing. We suffer through critiques about our freedom from men who have no use for freedom. We have standards—let us voice them.

Too many people, I think, have the Grand Inquisitor attitude regarding freedom. By this I refer to some of the greatest works ever written, by the Russian novelist Dostoevsky (1912, 1960). In these books, Dostoevsky reaches the pinnacle of his writing talent as he presents one of the most powerful and complex parables in literature. It is about a cardinal who is the Grand Inquisitor. He has burned 100 heretics the day before Jesus returns to earth in Seville, Spain, in the most terrible period of the Inquisition. Jesus appears before the crowd in front of the cathedral. The people recognize him, and he performs miracles. Then the Grand Inquisitor has him seized and thrown into prison.

The Grand Inquisitor comes to visit Jesus in prison, threatens to burn him, and says that he has no right to come back. Now everything is in the Church's hands. Jesus, during his first coming, told men that he would make them free, but men did not want to become free. "In the end they will lay their freedom at our feet and say to us, 'Make us your slaves, but feed us.'"

The Inquisitor and his Church have vanquished freedom in order to make men happy. The Inquisitor continues, "Man was created a rebel; and how can rebels be happy?" People suffer when they must choose between good and evil. They will gladly give up such suffering by letting others make their choices for them. Freedom brings unrest, confusion and unhappiness. The Inquisitor reveals that his Church has corrected God's work by establishing miracle, mystery and authority, and the people are happy to be led like sheep. He tells Jesus, "We shall have an answer for all. And they will be glad to believe our answer, for it will save them from the great anxiety and terrible agony they endure at present in making a free decision for themselves." Dostoevsky is saying that freedom is an act of faith. It is a divine gift, and the most precious property of people— given not by reason nor by science nor by natural law. He believed it was human nature not to want to be free—that people regard freedom as a curse.

What does the Grand Inquisitor legend say to those of us who are wondering if freedom is worth the price or whether it might be better to sell out its liberties to the cause of peace and bread and happiness? I believe that it is a warning to us. It says, "Let no siren song of comfort, happiness or plenty smudge the fact of God's image in people." The people who are free are free *indeed*.

Captured, a people become part of a herd. Freedom releases the energies of a people; tyranny kills them. In our struggle for a better life, we toss our manhood and our womanhood on the altar of Big Brother and accept direction of our social existence. We are only sowing the seeds thereby of another uprising of men and women who will sense, however dimly, that all people are created equal, endowed by their creator with certain inalienable rights. If there is anyone here who does not realize what happens to a people in this situation, I offer my experience in finding out the hard way. Unfortunately we have many examples of terror today. I can refer you to one of the very horrible examples in history. It's recorded by Alexander Solzhenitsyn in *The Gulag Archipelago* (1974). If you can't read the entire two volumes, as a sometime professor I give you your assignment for today. Read the first 100 pages of the first volume, or at least read through the arrest. At this point I recall what Winston Churchill said during World War II. When he was asked why they were fighting, he said, "Quit fighting and you'll find out."

I believe the heart of freedom is basically ethical and spiritual. It involves self-discipline and devotion to duty, truth, honor and respect. Ethically we must realize that a people and a nation do not do freely and voluntarily that which is right. The sacrifice and death of millions on the field of battle or the enactment of a million laws in the halls of Congress will not save freedom. Preserving freedom depends upon what each of us does every day.

Our heroic dead died not that we might do as we damn well please, but that we might do what is our high duty—what we ought to do. True freedom is not the freedom to do as we please; it is the power to do as we ought. We must learn one thing, and it is a hard lesson—to deny ourselves. We don't sufficiently emphasize self-denial and self-discipline either for ourselves or for our children. Instead we concentrate on our wants—on doing as we please and getting what we want. To learn to get along without, to realize that what our country is going to demand of us may be much more important than what we are entitled to demand of it—this, indeed, is a hard lesson.

Relative to self-discipline and the training of officers, many of you here today realize that the chic of permissiveness and the great turn-off over Vietnam have rendered ROTC training out of fashion in many places. So it is hardly surprising that the three military academies are suffering from the national virus of lack of self-discipline. They are experiencing an overwhelming attrition rate (from 36 to 46 percent). A substantial amount of this attrition is due to cheating. The common alibi is the familiar, "Everybody's doing it, and the academic competition is too tough." Yes, self-discipline is the price of freedom. And the test of freedom is not so much what we are free to do, but what we are free not to do. One of the best illustrations of this is again from Solzhenitsyn, in *One Day in The Life of Ivan Denisovich* (1963), which is also required reading. Alyoshka's freedom had nothing to do with guards, barbed wire, or the horrible conditions in the Siberian prison camp. It was inside of him, God-given and permanent. This example brings out the spiritual aspect of freedom.

I close this portion on freedom with two quotes. This first one is from Edmund Burke (1989): "Men are qualified for civil liberty in exact proportion to their disposition to put moral chains upon their own appetites....It is ordained in the eternal constitution of things, that men of intemperate minds cannot be free. Their passions forge their fetters." The second one is from Epictetus: "No man is free who is not master of himself."

Now we turn to integrity—about truth and sacred honor. Truth and honor are fading qualities both for our nation and for many of its people. These can only be kept bright by sacrifice and by devotion to duty. But erosion has set in; corruption has occurred. In this regard, I am not only thinking about the public office holders who have betrayed their trust, like our former president and his associates including a vice president and a couple of attorney generals, but also about the police officers who accept bribes, and the building and grain inspectors who obtain illegal commissions. These trouble me greatly. But something that is even more troublesome to me is the corruption of our everyday citizen. A wise man was once asked, "Why is a wildcat a wildcat?" He answered, "Because his mother and father are wildcats."

Everyday people on the street are corrupt—and that's you and me. Children, I am afraid, too often learn from their parents to cheat the telephone company, the storekeeper, the schools, and especially the government. I am also thinking of companies and corporations that cheat the consumer, bribe the officials, and do not level with the stockholders. Evidence for this corruption can be seen daily in the sale of shoddy merchandise, the performance of tax fraud openly and without remorse, the billing of Medicare and Medicaid for services that are not rendered, and the cheating of the elderly by some nursing homes. To me, these are the same as physical assault on a person. Our free enterprise system, which I was a part of for 15 years, has, I fear, often come to mean that people are free to grab all they can get for goods and services rendered. If it really means that, then our free enterprise system is not economic freedom but economic tyranny.

As we survey the contemporary scene, no one can deny that we as a people and a nation are in trouble. Some days I am at the point of despair; I feel that the great American dream that my parents came from Norway to be a part of has turned into a nightmare. But when I am almost to the point of losing faith in our republic, in our youth, in inherent decency, someone does something good. Someone makes the world better for having lived in it and thereby affects my life and the lives of those around me. At such times my faith in another very important ingredient of freedom—trust—is reaffirmed. I am grateful that I can enjoy a great amount of freedom because I trust my wife and she trusts me. I trust the man who runs the service station, because I know that he will do what is necessary for my car (and he knows that I don't know very much about it) and at a fair price. I trust my banker, my C.P.A. and my lawyer. I'm grateful that I can rely on these people; it gives me a great deal of freedom.

In closing, I believe that we as a people must face up far more honestly and resolutely to the many serious problems that confront us. We are in serious danger of losing basic freedoms today, not so much because of military threat or political pressure from outside, but because of our failure to fulfill the conditions of freedom that I have briefly discussed with you today. I believe history teaches us that the foundation of a republic's power is not restricted to its armies, but rests on the integrity of its institutions and its people. It is probably unnecessary for me to remind you that when integrity was lost in the Roman republic, Rome's decline became inevitable. Athens fell because its errors seemed so very sweet to its people that they didn't want to correct them. We must all come to realize that not all bondage is from the outside. We forge our own chains by our moral looseness, by our cynical acceptance of loose standards as the way things are, or by the excuse that everybody's doing it.

The message for today is that we must not lose hope. Admittedly there is, in many places, overwhelming repression; many people are yet imprisoned without charges and subjected to terrible torture. But there are encouraging signs—a foment for freedom in places we couldn't have imagined. We must continue to strive diligently and pray that political prisoners and prisoners of conscience be set free. I must admit to a deep concern, however, because our American constitutional democracy has been placed in great peril in recent decades. It seemed almost any situation called an emergency was considered reason enough for the executive branch to suspend the rights of its citizens, delegate powers to itself, and to otherwise distort or break the law or lie deliberately.

We have been poignantly reminded that great power can easily be abused, that if one powerful person is allowed to rise above the law, the law as a whole is placed in jeopardy. A heavy reliance on secrecy is incompatible with democracy. Current political, economic and philosophic conditions make it a time in which serious threats to liberty in American history could take place. My intention is to awaken our associates and ourselves and our nation to the realization that our democracy is a very fragile thing indeed, and without concern and nurture and continuing vigilance we stand to lose it.

The signatories of the Declaration of Independence signed their death warrant. They pledged their lives, their fortunes, and their sacred honor. By this I interpret that they equated their sacred honor with their lives, and you and I can do no less. We must, as a nation and as a people, strive to return to honor, to become more believable again. For you who are being commissioned today, I wish you well in this important assignment—because our very lives may depend upon it. This is best exemplified by my final quotation by a famous American who found out what the cost of freedom was:

> If a man happens to be 38 years old, as I happen to be, and some great truth stands before the door of his life, some great opportunity to stand up for that which is right and that which is just, and he refuses to stand up because he wants to live a little longer and he is afraid his home will get bombed, or he is afraid that he will get shot...he may go on and live until he's 80, and the cessation of breathing in his life is merely the belated announcement of an earlier death of the spirit.

> Man dies when he refuses to stand up for that which is right. A man dies when he refuses to take a stand for that which is true. So we are going to stand up right here...letting the world know we are determined to be free.

> *Martin Luther King, Jr., in a speech given at the Ebenezer Baptist Church, Atlanta, Georgia.*

This stand cost him his life. Millions believe it was worth it and honor him today as a great American.

The significant question for you and me is not "What's in it for me?" but "Why am I here?" And we answer that not with a word or two or even a sentence or a whole paragraph, but with a life dedicated to nurturing other people, animals, and our natural environment with compassion, reverence and integrity. If we are not here to do that, there is probably no just and sufficient reason to be here at all. As we take leave of one another, my prayer is that you and your children will not have to find out what freedom really means—the way I did—by losing it.

I wish you well.

Mike Hildebrand - First Recipient of Delta Society's President's Award

For more than a decade at Delta Society annual meetings, we have reviewed observations on many subjects; most prominent among these are the human-animal bond and animal-assisted therapy. Examples of these subjects "in action" are deemed very popular by the attendees. Impressive animal-person relationships and helpful interactions are singled out for awards. One of the more remarkable was Michael Hildebrand's involvement with a special horse named Dancer. Their relationship reflected the remarkable abilities of animals and their contribution to the health and well-being of people—most especially those who are disadvantaged or have disabilities.

Michael Hildebrand, a boy with Duchenne's muscular dystrophy, attended the annual Delta Conference in Vancouver, B.C. in 1987 to accept the President's Award from me. He was accompanied by his mother, Janice, and his grandmother, Elsie Hall, courtesy of the Dream Factory. This award is presented to the team that best exemplifies the power of the bond between people and animals and the joy each brings to the life of the other.

Mike was a very bright and gifted lad. Before he was 9 years old, he was severely affected by Duchenne's muscular dystrophy. The failure of his body strength also caused severe depression in both body and spirit. Then enter "A Bit o' Heaven Irish Dancer," a wonderful horse which had its own history of disability. Laura Carpenter, a trainer par excellence, put Mike on Dancer, and a wonderful and rewarding bond developed. Dancer was ridden nearly exclusively by Michael from 1984 to 1987 in the therapeutic horsemanship classes at Three Creek Farm in St. Charles, Missouri.

"Dancer's intuition of what Mike wanted when he rode approached mind reading," said Sandy Rafferty, founder of the therapeutic horseback riding program. As Mike's condition deteriorated, Dancer compensated for the changes and did well at interpreting his commands.

As a result, Mike was able to continue riding with a surprising degree of independence. Although Dancer carried all of her previous riders with responsive patience, she particularly delighted and consoled Mike.

In August of 1985, Mike went to Augusta, Michigan, to compete in the National Association of Sports for Cerebral Palsy. He and Dancer won three gold medals in equitation, dressage, and obstacle course. All that stood between Mike and the conviction of his own helplessness was Dancer. "She made his life an adventure," said Laura Carpenter. "Sometimes when I watched Dancer carry Mike so carefully around the ring, I believed she knew that she had enriched his life remarkably."

Although Mike's condition in 1987 was deteriorating, he was hoping to compete once more—in San Francisco—but the meet was canceled which was a big disappointment. However, when Mike heard he was to receive this award his spirits were buoyed. He and his mother and grandmother were met at the Vancouver airport by a very large limousine and array of balloons, and they arrived in great style at the hotel where they had a lovely suite of rooms. Mike did a demonstration ride, and he was interviewed for television and by newspaper reporters. At the awards banquet he was the last recipient, and I recounted some of Mike's history before introducing him. He responded with these remarkable words:

> Every hour of every day
> Three hundred sixty-five days a year,
> I ride.
> I ride in a blue and silver wheelchair.
> It bothers me when people stare,
> But maybe they really do care.
> There are many things I can't do.
> Wouldn't this upset you, too?
> One and a half hours a day,
> About fifty-two days a year,
> I ride.
> I ride on a dark brown Connemara.
> Dancer is my very best friend.
> Upon her I often depend.
> Without wheels, she makes me feel free!
> That's all I really want to be.

When Mike accepted the award and recited his poem, the audience "tasted salt" as they gave him a standing ovation. These words were from his unpublished autobiography, entitled *The Springtime of My Life*, and spring was all he had in his life because he died seven months later. But before Mike died, Dr. Earl Strimple, a veterinarian and a member of the Delta Society Board of Directors, not only sent science fiction books and letters to Mike, he informed one of his clients, Senator John Danforth, of Mike's story since Mike was from Missouri, too. Senator Danforth expressed all of our feelings in the following letter:

Dear Mike,

What a great sense of accomplishment and pride you must feel to have received the President's Award of the Delta Society.

Dr. Strimple has told me of your wonderful success with Dancer. It must give you a great sense of satisfaction to have become such a proficient rider. But I am sure you know that your accomplishment extends way beyond yourself. It stands as a beacon of hope for everyone who must overcome an obstacle in the quest of excellence. What a great message for you to give to the rest of the world: all dreams are possible if they are pursued with faith and dedication.

You are an inspirational young man. I want you to know that I am so proud of you. My prayers are with you

Your Friend,

John Danforth

And so ends the all too short but beautiful story of the remarkable abilities of animals and the compassionate love and understanding manifest between people, and between people and animals.

Nurtured Children:
An Endangered Species?

Recently, we had a very rewarding experience in a kindergarten class (observing was a visitor from Japan who was here to learn about our People-Pet Partnership Program and about Delta Society's resources and outreach). Terry Ryan—then Program Coordinator of People-Pet Partnership, now president of her own company, Legacy, consultants on animal training and behavior—assisted by Michelle, a student volunteer from the College of Engineering, and Molly, a basset hound, presented a dog-bite prevention lesson to the morning and afternoon kindergarten students. Molly belongs to Joe and Charlene Douglas. Molly has passed the American Kennel Club Canine Good Citizenship test and met the requirements of Delta's Pet Partners program. On arriving for the afternoon session and walking down the hallway to the classroom, they met one of the students from the morning class. Terry then intervened and asked the boy to show his mother what he had learned. Without hesitation, he went through the whole procedure—perfectly, much to the amazement and satisfaction of Terry, the child, the child's mother and Michelle, the volunteer. And it certainly impressed our Japanese visitor, Dr. Kono, and his interpreter, Seiichi Murai. And it impressed me when Michelle returned to our office with the dog and enthusiastically related her experiences of the day with the children and the dog.

For many years, I've admired the accomplishments of one of our country's leading psychiatrists, David Hamburg. He is president of the Carnegie Corporation. His annual report arrived recently and it has something important to say about educating children. He urges that "deliberate explicit emphasis" be placed on developing "prosocial" attributes in the young. He went on to state that "taking turns, sharing and cooperating—these norms, established early in life, can open the way to beneficial human relations that can have significance throughout adulthood extending to membership in larger units, possibly including international relations." He went on to state that "the painfully difficult effort to achieve decent, fair and peaceful relations among diverse human groups is an enterprise that must be renewed." In his appeal for non-violent resolution, Dr. Hamburg directed some special remarks to families, schools, community organi-

First published in slightly longer form in *The Caring Communiqué* vol. 1 no. 1, 1994.

zations and the media, which he said have the power to "shape attitudes and inter-personal skills toward either decent relations or hatred and violence."

In reading Dr. Hamburg's well-chosen words, I recalled a conversation I had in Japan with the "king" of psychiatrists and others. At the invitation of the Japanese Animal Hospital Association, I discussed the benefits that can accrue to children who have properly selected companion animals. The Pet Education Partnership instructional program developed by the People-Pet Partnership includes live animal classroom presentations on choosing and caring for pets and the owners' responsibilities, and has been translated into Japanese.

I noted that, in many countries, there are people who are very concerned about the well-being of animals and their importance to people's health. We have much to learn from animals. They, like very young children, have a common language; territorial boundaries are not important impediments to communication, interchange or in building community. Children and animals are, I believe, an excellent basis for our international peace initiative and could serve as a basis for dialogue on peace by all nations. I believe such action could help Dr. Hamburg fulfill some of his recommendations.

I brought this subject up during my visit to Japan in July, 1988. Keiko Yamazaki organized a special luncheon to which she invited people with diverse backgrounds. Among other subjects, I mentioned my thoughts on a peace initiative. I reiterated that animals, people with disabilities and the elderly suffer most in war and are an excellent basis for our international peace initiative. Dr. H. Akimoto, often referred to as the "king" of psychiatry in Japan, enthusiastically joined in on the conversation. He felt strongly that children and animals were an appropriate basis for dialogue for neither had difficulty in communicating, nor did they find national or state borders any obstacle for interaction.

I propose that such an interaction would bring diverse peoples together on common ground in an atmosphere of love and peace. It would be an opportunity to share important scientific and cultural information and would also have tremendous potential for promoting positive international public relations. In short, it would be "animal-assisted therapy" on a global scale! The theme might be "People-Pets-Peace," which could serve as a basis for dialogue on peace by many nations. On leaving this luncheon meeting, I was pleased that my host on this visit seemed to feel strongly about such an initiative. Although such an initiative may not be implemented in my lifetime, I hope and pray it will occur during the lifetime of many people who read this and join the Dance of Peace by children all over the world.

Children are an endangered "species." It grieves me deeply that, while children should be a top priority, many are suffering and dying. Although we are considered to be the richest nation in the world, 14.6 million of our children lived in poverty in 1992 (latest census figures), which is five million more than 21 years earlier. Recent estimates reveal that approximately 2.7 million children are reported as victims of abuse and neglect in the U.S. annually. It is estimated that three million children witness parental violence every year; and a child is reported abused or neglected every thirteen seconds and those reports continue to climb. The number of reports has almost tripled since 1980.

Children are not only increasingly being victimized by violence, but countless numbers of them witness or lose loved ones to violence. They are being subjected to physical injuries, emotional or sexual maltreatment and deprivation of necessities. Child abuse and neglect are part of a complex web of family violence, including cruelty to animals.

Current research confirms that animal abuse by children and juveniles may be a predictor of current and future antisocial behavior that escalates against human beings. Cruelty to animals is implicated in various forms of family and community violence. Unfortunately, many of these victimized children are left alone to wrestle with their fears and grief without adequate counseling or treatment by mental health professionals who are trained to relieve chronic endangerment. We are witnessing a breakdown in American values, common sense and parental and community responsibility for nurturing and protecting children. We need a greater investment in their early years as a key crime prevention strategy. We are bankrupting the hope of our children.

Children who have suffered from violence and the threat of it may well suffer permanent disability from such experiences. What is needed is a commitment to normalization of the damage to such tender, innocent victims. Some of the children suffer from post-traumatic stress disorder, which is very bad news—and I say this from first-hand experience.

Intervention with carefully selected companion animals could well help in normalization, providing nurturance and suitable objects of nurture; and this intervention could make a difference and should no longer be trivialized. I must say that I'm disappointed that Sigmund Freud failed to capitalize on his observations on his dog. Sigmund Freud said this about his dog, a Chow Chow named Jo-Fi:

> Affectionate without ambivalence, the simplicity of a life free from almost unbearable conflicts in civilization, the beauty of existence complete in itself and yet, despite all divergences in organic development [there is] that feeling of intimate affinity, of an undisputed solidarity...a bond of friendship united us both....

Freud was also reputed to have said: "In bringing up children, all you do is wrong!" Freud, we've learned, not only had Jo-Fi—who he said understood what a particular patient needed better than he did—but a series of dogs. In his practice, his dogs were always at his feet, even while he was counseling.

I'll readily admit that I have admiration and respect for James H.S. Bossard, a sociologist at the University of Pennsylvania who published a paper fifty years ago in the journal *Mental Hygiene* entitled "The Mental Hygiene of Owning a Dog." "This article is written to present the thesis that domestic animals play an important role in family life and in the mental health of its members, with particular reference to children in the family." He was amazed by the response to his article by people from seemingly all walks of life. He recounted this in an article in 1950, the first sentence of which was: "The role of domestic animals as household pets, their importance as a factor in family relations in general and in mental hygiene in particular, seems to be strongly neglected in the serious literature in these respective fields."

There is considerable evidence and many suggestions, such as that by Bossard, that should encourage many people in several disciplines to perform definitive studies. I will admit that, at long last, there seems to be a change in the attitudes of some people regarding the importance of animals in the lives of people. Twenty years ago, a report on the human-animal bond was regarded as soft science at best and speculations about warm fuzzies from the funny farm.

A recent issue of the *Harvard Newsletter* from Harvard Medical School gave front page coverage to "Pets and Health—A Friend Indeed." It was a reasonable treatment covering some of the recent reports on the beneficial effects of human-animal interactions. I'm looking forward to an expansion and broad reception and acceptance in this area, since some of the world leaders in child and family studies are addressing the issue of children's interaction with animals in schools, hospitals, prisons and institutions for people with disabilities.

At a time when adult nurturers are needed more than ever by our society, the children's opportunities for giving and receiving nurturing seem to be diminishing. There is a need for nurturers, for there are countless children throughout the world and here in the United States who are being starved in body, soul and spirit, abused, molested and lacking nurture. To provide a healthy, nurturing environment for all of the children of the world must be our number one priority. By respecting that priority and involving companion animals, we can assure a better world tomorrow.

Bumper stickers sometimes manifest creativity and great truths. The one I saw coming to work is very apropos: "A world of wanted children would make a world of difference!" It is only those who love and nurture their children who can share the joy of the spontaneous delight they manifest. Their laughter must not be allowed to be tainted by cynicism and superiority, but be the laughter of the pure in heart who recognize when life is fun and funny, which is often enhanced by a companion animal. For many children, there is no joy, no fun. We must restore that with great haste!

Acknowledgments

The work and helpful suggestions of Daun Martin, Pam Barker, Charlene Douglas, and Signe Bustad of People-Pet Partnership and Mary Ellen Radziemski and associates in the Child Care Center are gratefully acknowledged.

The Importance Of Animals To The Well-Being Of People

This is a subject in which I have invested a great deal of effort and resources over the past two decades. And I have committed the rest of my days to it. They have been a very reward-ing two decades, principally because of the many capable, wonderful people I have met who are devoted to contributing to the well-being of people, animals and the environment.

I used an invitation from the American Animal Hospital Association to submit a manuscript on this subject to pay tribute to a very dear friend and associate in the Delta Society and in our Northwest Regional Program in Veterinary Medicine. Michael J. McCulloch, M.D., was a remarkable human being whose contributions and influence nationally and internationally were nothing short of phenomenal. We are grateful for his life and work with us; we miss him terribly!

This presentation is an abbreviated version of what was published in the American Animal Hospital Association's (AAHA) publication, Trends (Bustad, 1985), and we appreciate AAHA's permission to include it in this book.

It is with a heavy heart, but also with great hope, that I write this article chiefly because of the life and recent death of an uncommon man and dear friend, Dr. Michael McCulloch. This article is dedicated to him and his pioneering work. A few brief quotations from the *Congressional Record* of Thursday, July 18, 1985, entitled "Memorial for Dr. Michael McCulloch," sum-marize well his life and his work. Senator Proxmire said:

> Mr. President, exceptional men deserve recognition. Particularly when their life works enrich all of us....Dr. Michael McCulloch was an exceptional man.

> Friends, acquaintances, and relatives describe him as a devoted fam-ily man, deeply caring for his wife, his four children, and a nephew who was welcomed to the family following the tragic loss of his parents.

> Colleagues and patients describe him as conscientious, profes-sional, sensitive. "An able physician," "a leader in psychiatry," a man whose "quiet suggestions" made a real difference in the lives of those he touched.

His training in psychiatry gave him a special understanding of human behavior. His love of animals, beginning at an early age, made him keenly aware of the special affinities between people and animals. He believed, recalled his brother, Dr. William McCulloch, that through medicine he could help people, and through knowledge of people-animal relationships, he could improve the healing art....

To understand the human-companion animal bond, McCulloch called for a disciplined effort by scientists from several fields and initiated his own careful studies.

In 1977 he helped establish the Delta Society to study human/animal relationships and how they may be used to facilitate therapy. The society grew; its membership spread across the United States and drew from many disciplines. It became the leading professional organization conducting research on the effect of animals on human health, initiating companion animal programs for disturbed children, handicapped persons, prisoners, and patients in hospitals and nursing homes; and educating Americans about the benefits of human-animal interaction. The research and education activities of the Delta Society played a key role in securing passage of the pets in elderly housing bill which I introduced in 1983.

This legislation prohibits discrimination against elderly or handicapped persons who wish to have a pet companion and who live in federally funded housing. It reflects recent research findings that pet ownership can significantly improve the physical and emotional health of older or handicapped people.

Those who heard Dr. McCulloch speak about the bonds that link humans and companion animals recognized him as an exceptional communicator. He marshaled his information about human psychology, medicine, and animal behavior carefully. He conveyed complex matter with professional clarity. He described the wondrous results of human/animal interactions with a quiet, but convincing passion. Both in his lectures and in his writings, Dr. McCulloch revealed himself as an uncommon teacher.

On the morning of Wednesday, June 26, Dr. McCulloch was shot to death in his office by a deranged former patient.

He will be missed. The loss will be felt not only by his family, his friends, and others who knew him. This exceptional man, who worked so hard to increase our understanding of the bonds which link all living creatures, and to use this knowledge to cure those who are ill and comfort those who cannot be cured, will be remembered by all of us.

I am deeply grateful for all he did to enrich my life, that of my family, our college, profession and our society.

A decade ago, I wrote an article entitled "Pets-For-People Therapy" in which I discussed the benefits of companion animals. I proposed their use in a number of situations, such as placement in local nursing and convalescent homes, a project we had already begun. I explained in this article that animals could improve the psychological well-being of countless people. In the intervening ten years, I have traveled extensively and learned of the experiences and studies of many people reported at a variety of meetings, including three international conferences. I am now even more convinced that animals, properly selected and maintained, can contribute to the health and well-being of many more people—not only psychologically, but physically and socially. More and more health professionals will be recommending that people obtain animals as companions or as helpers. In this regard, Tom Ferguson, M.D., quoted me in his article "Medical Self Care": "I believe the day is coming when doctors will sometimes 'prescribe' pets instead of pills....What pill gives so much love, makes one feel safe, stimulates laughter, encourages regular exercise and makes a person feel needed?"

This day is already here! In this brief article I believe I can best express my feelings by telling you what I would do if I were dictator. The following is taken from (slightly modified) the summary I presented at the International Symposium on Human-Pet Relationships, honoring the 80th birthday of Nobel Laureate Konrad Lorenz in Vienna, Austria in 1983, which I prepared with the help of Dr. Michael McCulloch and others:

"In jest I have often stated what I would do if I were a dictator. In concluding this meeting, I am, on the basis of what I have learned here these past two days as well as my experiences over the past decade, telling you what I would do relative to the human-animal bond if I were dictator:

"1. The first thing I would do is to incorporate into the curriculum of all school systems, including universities, courses on the human-animal bond. It would begin at a very early age; as a result, within one generation we could have responsible pet care as the 'rule,' rather than as the exception it is now in our society. The course offerings would be designed to improve the selection process for choosing companion animals, thereby remarkably improving the strength of the bond in a variety of situations. A course on 'Reverence for Life' modeled after the one I teach at Washington State University would be required. This would hopefully raise the sensitivity level of future generations so they will not consider animals as 'throw-away' items, but will take killing seriously.

"2. The second thing I would give special emphasis to as dictator is a subject I have already alluded to, and that is improved selection of animals. In our experience, the failure to experience a positive human-companion animal relationship, a healthy and rewarding bond, is the poor selection of animal (and recipient). This, along with the ignorance on the part of the recipient, portend a disastrous relationship. As we progress we must develop better selection criteria that may well include setting up special breeding programs for appropriate 'therapy animals.'

"3. As dictator I would have veterinarians assist in facilitating the proper selection and placement of pets and insuring the health and welfare of every animal. As important members of a team approach to animal-assisted therapy, veterinarians could contribute to development of a scientific profile and scoring system for dogs that would aid in their appropriate selection and placement. Such scoring could also be used in evaluating qualitatively and, hopefully, quantitatively the effect on the animal from its use in various situations with a variety of patients. From such dedicated effort could come immeasurable happiness and well-being for both animals and people.

"4. As dictator, I would install aquaria in all dental and medical offices, elementary school classrooms, and conference rooms and lunch rooms of all businesses, institutions, prisons, schools and governmental offices. All interviewing rooms would have as residents one or more docile, friendly animals. Similar animals would also be appropriately housed in student dormitories, nursing and convalescent homes.

"5. Hospitals would have assigned wards where patients who require their animals to accompany them when they go to the hospital would be accommodated. Hospices would have provisions for accepting terminal patients and their companion animals, and terminal patients would have an animal available if they wished to have one. All hospital forms will be modified to include two additional questions: 'If you live alone, do you own a pet or pets?' and, 'Who should be called to care for them in emergencies?'

"6. Appropriate guidelines would be established and respected for companion animals in nursing and convalescent homes, retirement homes and all government housing. Hopefully, they would be extended to privately owned housing as well.

"7. Animal programs would be implemented in all penal institutions. The objectives would be the education of the prisoners and their provision of useful service to the community. Service could include training specially selected animals to help people with handicaps, nursing injured or diseased wildlife back to health, and obedience training of selected animals from animal control centers so they would be better companion animals after adoption.

"8. Subsidized pet care programs, possibly government sponsored, would be established to provide health care for animals vital to the well-being of low-income people.

"9. Disaster plans that include provisions for evacuation and care of animals as well as people would be implemented.

"10. In most households, at least two companion animals of different ages would be recommended, especially in single person households and with the elderly and people with disabilities.

"11. Any new buildings would be constructed to accommodate not only the elderly and people with handicaps, but also companion animals. Park facilities would also be constructed so as to address the needs of companion animals and their owners.

"12. As dictator, I would establish a very generous research fund to support promising proposals on the human-animal bond. This addresses the most urgent need voiced by the Delta Society, i.e., careful investigations. This is the basic tenet not only of the Delta Society but, as I understand it, of all the official human-animal bond societies sponsoring this symposium including AFIRAC of France, IEMT of Austria, JACOPIS in Australia and SCAS of the U.K.

"13. As dictator, I would establish animal care facilities in certain industries and business establishments. I've made this suggestion for several reasons. Many single people who live alone have one or more pets; often it's a single dog that has to be placed in a kennel every day or left home alone all day. It would be far better for the animal and its owner to be able to bring the dog to work every day. The dog could be visited during breaks and taken for a run at noon. Information sessions and dog obedience instruction could also be arranged for the noon hour or after work. Cooperative programs could be developed with children in day care centers at these establishments. Such programs could involve instruction of children on the care of, and interaction with, dogs and other animals. Health benefits to children interacting with carefully selected pets have been shown. Provisions for grief therapy could also be provided for both employees and children (and animals)."

More and more people are recognizing the extent to which pets can facilitate therapy for an assortment of human problems. They provide security and comfort for older people, positive focus for those who are in prisons, and important therapy for those who have serious disabilities. Veterinarians should continue to work toward the adoption of laws that would permit the use of pets in institutions in each of our states rather than denying people who reside in institutions this remarkable source of comfort and help.

On the basis of experiences by many people and institutions in Australia, Europe, New Zealand and North America, companion animals must be recognized as vital to the physical, psychological and social well-being of people and as agents of therapy in a great number of conditions and situations. Almost everyone could benefit by contact with warm "fuzzies" (unless we are allergic), and our companion animals offer us security, succor, esteem, understanding, forgiveness, fun and laughter and, most importantly, abundant and unconditional love. Furthermore, they make no judgments, and we can be ourselves with them. They also need our help and make us feel important.

I close with a statement from Dr. Michael McCulloch's presentation on animal-assisted therapy at the International Conference on the Human-Animal Bond at the University of Pennsylvania, October, 1981: "If pet therapy offers hope for relief of human suffering, it is our professional obligation to explore every available avenue for its use."

Excellence In Teaching
In An Established School:
Are We Still "Stuck"
With The Saber-Tooth Curriculum?

On several occasions I have addressed suggested changes in the veterinary curricula. But changes are usually resisted. The power of the status quo is formidable. This is best exemplified in a remarkable book, The Saber-Tooth Curriculum, by J. Abner Peddiwell (pseudonym of Harold Benjamin, 1939). I was invited to address the subject of "An Historic Perspective of Veterinary Medical Education" at a national conference at which I discussed some of Peddiwell's ideas. As I examined the history of veterinary medical curricula starting at the first veterinary schools in France in the mid 1700s, I was struck by the fact that there have been extended periods of time when one could leave a veterinary college for several decades (would you believe a century?) and return only to find the curricula and course offerings relatively unchanged. Curricular change is, and has always been, difficult to implement (but that may not be all bad), and Peddiwell helped me understand why.

In the 1700s it was considered quite remarkable that some eminent physicians recognized the need for veterinary education. Two of the earliest proponents in the human medical community for the study of veterinary science were the famous physician Benjamin Rush and a fellow member of the Philadelphia Society for Promoting Agriculture, Dr. James Mease. This society went on record advocating veterinary medicine. Among its members were George Washington, Benjamin Franklin, Noah Webster and Judge Richard Peters. Judge Peters appears to be the first public figure to call for the establishment of a veterinary profession in America. (Significantly, George Washington manifested exemplary conduct regarding animals. Judge Peters said that Washington "commenced every day with a visit to his stables in which he minutely examined and directed every necessary arrangement: and no person of his day knew better how to treat the horse.") Because of his exemplary performance, I recommended that we confer an honorary DVM degree on the father of our country, George Washington—especially since he seems to have suffered no damage from the treason trial with which he was threatened in London in 1990.

Presentation to the Military Surgeons in Washington, D.C., November, 1978.

When the subject of excellence comes up, the discussion usually gets around to curriculum because that's something tangible and everybody knows what it should contain. However, there is never a unanimity of opinion except that you need one. Although I've had a long-term interest in curriculum, I lacked knowledge about it when I was appointed dean of the College of Veterinary Medicine at Washington State University in 1973. But as a scientist, I did what any good scientist does—go to the library and see what's been done. I was lucky I found a remarkable book that I remembered was published when I was an undergraduate: *The Saber-Tooth Curriculum* by J. Abner Peddiwell (1939).

Peddiwell's book tells about the first educational theorist and practitioner. His name was New Fist Hammermaker, but everyone called him New Fist. He lived in the Paleolithic Era. New Fist was a thinker and a doer which was a threat to many people then, as it is now. He wanted a better life for his people: more and better food, clothing and security, and more leisure. He strove for excellence, so he established what is considered to be the first program in systematic education. He set up the first curriculum, and *he stuck to the basics*:

- Fish grabbing with the bare hands
- Woolly horse clubbing
- Saber-tooth tiger scaring with fire

Now probably everybody here says that makes sense because this was his culture, and these were the three basic needs. But this was not true for New Fist. Two great pressure groups descended on him: (1) Those that said he was trying to change human nature and everybody knows you can't change human nature; and (2) those in organized religion that said he was going against common religious beliefs—for if the Great Mystery had intended for children to pursue the three activities of his curriculum, he would have given them natural instincts to perform these functions. But New Fist was also an educational statesman, and he replied to both groups politely with reason. After that it wasn't long before everyone in the tribe knew the heart of a good education lay in the three basics of the curriculum:

- Fish Grabbing
- Horse Clubbing
- Tiger Scaring

And this worked for a generation or so, and it worked well. But then a great change came. A new Ice Age was coming, and as the great glacier approached, the water in the streams became muddy and educated people couldn't see to catch fish with their bare hands. And as if that wasn't bad enough, the dumb woolly horses left the country because of the change in weather and were replaced by a small, speedy, agile antelope that no one could get close enough to club like they could with the woolly horses. Even worse, the saber-tooth tigers all caught pneumonia and, in the absence of veterinarians, became weak and died and were replaced by big bears who were mean. They roamed not only at night, but by day, and they weren't frightened by fire.

The tribe faced a crisis—a crisis in curriculum and a crisis in their way of life.

But some ingenious descendants of New Fist invented fish nets to catch fish in muddy streams. Others developed antelope snares, and still others prepared camouflaged bear pits. I'm here to tell you this new technology caught on and prosperity and security returned, but it took some doing to get it into the educational apparatus. Some of the technologists began to ask, "Why can't net making, snare setting and bear-pit digging be taught in school?" "Why?" asked the radicals. "Well," said the old educators, "because it's mere training, and our standard curriculum of *fish grabbing, horse clubbing and tiger scaring* is too crowded now. There's no room for fads and frills!" The wise old educators smiled benignly and said, "That wouldn't be education." "But, damn it all," said the radicals, "how can any thinking person be interested in useless activities like fish grabbing, horse clubbing and tiger scaring?"

"Foolishness!" said the traditionalists. "We don't teach fish grabbing to grab fish! We teach it to develop generalized agility which can't be developed by mere practical training. We don't teach horse clubbing to club horses! We teach it to develop generalized strength that you'll never get in a course in antelope snaring! And we don't teach tiger scaring to scare tigers! We teach it to impart courage which extends into all aspects of life, something you can't gain in a crude course in bear-pit digging!"

But the radicals persisted. "Why not try a change in the curriculum to address these new needs?" The traditionalists became indignant and said, "If you had any appreciation for education, you would know that the essence of true education is timelessness! You youngsters must come to realize there are some eternal truths that endure through changing conditions like solid granite in a raging stream. And, furthermore, these eternal truths are uniquely inherent in *our* saber-tooth curriculum."

This discussion of the saber-tooth curriculum emphasizes the hazards of status quo. It is hazardous because flexibility and receptiveness to new ideas and change are necessary to achieve excellence, even though it is innate in most people to resist change because change challenges one's security. Progress, however, cannot be realized in the absence of change. I hasten to add, however, that change is not necessarily equated to progress. Often change means retrogression. Changes need to occur, but the decision to change should not be arrived at lightly. In every possible case, change should only occur after much study and wise counsel.

I must also point out that the status quo is also hazardous because it can lead to apathy—even though apathy has a lot going for it, according to an article in a newsletter sent to us by the U.S. Chamber of Commerce. It is easy to catch, and it's painless. You can ignore it and nothing happens. The stronger it gets, the less you feel you need to do something about it. It becomes noticeable when it begins to spread over a large area. When it does, the individual usually feels it belongs to someone else.

Another appealing thing about apathy is the warm glow of nothingness it gives. The temptation is to leave it alone, and it will go away. With this attitude it may stay. Apathy demands a special treatment, for it will not go away alone. The treatment starts with a good dose of involvement followed by long periods of action. It may be hard to get a confirmed apathetic to take the cure. And then it isn't permanent.

Action must be rewarded, while apathy is to be condemned. Since it is easier to condemn than to praise, however, it stands to reason that apathy is here to stay. It is needed by those who would rather condemn than act. Apathy has a lot going for it, but action is more fun. It must be. Have you ever heard anyone say, "Let's go where the apathy is?"

Action may not lead to excellence, but where there's excellence there's action. Yes, if an established university is to attain and maintain excellence it must always be actively striving, maintaining flexibility, challenging and demanding more from faculty and students, and adding new faculty. It must also be actively promoting self-development programs of present faculty, seeking better ways of presenting information, but never neglecting the basics as appropriately defined.

I usually keep these words on the top of my blackboard: "Success is never final. Failure need not be." Success and excellence for any college will require hard work and continual striving. People were made to strive! In this regard, I recall for you the great words penned by Sir Geoffrey Vickers:

> For each of us as well as for society and posterity, the need to struggle is the chance to grow. The world is like a dark forge, lighted by sparks which men strike as they beat the stuff of life into significance on the anvil of circumstance. The light is a function of the effort; we make it as bright as day if we hammer hard enough; but we shall never dispense with the need to hammer or live by the light of the sparks struck yesterday.

We are not made only for leisure; leisure is to refresh us so we may be better workers. Improvements of our situation are principally "borne on the swiftly beating wings of great desire." Related to this discussion is an observation I made a long time ago, and it is this: One of the greatest deterrents to attaining excellence is the 40-hour week. Excellence in any university will never be achieved in a 40-hour week on the part of faculty and students.

Excellence requires us to respect science and uncertainty. I believe science courses, especially in the fields of medicine, must have a strong input of associated experience and must recognize medicine as a human enterprise. Otherwise, the price we pay in our educational processes is a failure in the development of clinical judgment and compassionate wisdom in our students and a slowness in gaining practical appreciation and useful working knowledge in both the science and art of animal health care delivery. Let me expand on this concern. I believe that too often in our educational programs we inculcate an expectancy of certainty of knowledge and an aversion and an intolerance for uncertainty. To foster the expectation of certainty of knowledge is a serious betrayal of the essence of the scientific method and movement. In this regard, I believe we have been using the wrong punctuation marks. It is wrong to symbolize science with a period signifying finality. It is far more appropriate to *symbolize science with a question mark* signifying doubt, the need for a further look. It is the question mark, not the period, that best represents science as a powerful force for progress in our profession.

Too often, too many students in too many courses are forced by dogmatic teachers to accept science as a set of facts. I believe we must continue to develop in our students a great tolerance for uncertainties, and a more adventurous and enthusiastic curiosity about some of the bigger questions that characterize our professional field. Frankly, you and I and most students are uncomfortable with uncertainty. But at the risk of discomfort, we must "tell it like it is" and admit to uncertainties.

Most of the scientific community has shied away from studying or teaching animal and human nature and behavior because it is "unscientific," meaning, of course, unsatisfactorily deterministic and marked with uncertainty. They counsel anyone with scientific aspirations to turn away from such questionable adventures and to devote attention to more gratifying and respected areas where certain knowledge is available in large supply.

We do not imply that scientific facts and concepts are not important. Basic information in our curriculum is like the multiplication tables; it must be learned, memorized and used frequently to prevent disuse atrophy. But we need a greater appreciation for science in the broader perspective as well, stressing stimulation of critical thinking, problem solving and intellectual curiosity, and we need to inculcate this in all students.

The bottom line for any program of excellence is excellent people. Neither modern facilities nor quality equipment, vital though they are, can substitute for people who are bright, honest, well-trained, dedicated and committed to teaching, research, service and quality scholarship.

And this brings me to my final point which is intimately involved in this bottom line. It is mandatory that we instill a sense of ethics and professionalism in our graduates. This necessitates dealing with questions of ethics and professional norms and behavior as part of the curricula of veterinary colleges. Certainly, human medicine has already taken the lead in curricular innovations in this area. At many schools of medicine today, students have courses and seminars in a range of topics from medical and ethical issues to physician-patient role responsibilities. These courses have a varied format, including classroom instruction and interviews or discussions in the clinical settings.

In veterinary medicine it is our responsibility to do something about the ethical compass of our students whom we are privileged to teach. We can do something about this in our curriculum and we must. But there's another way that is far more important and it doesn't involve a sentence or two, a paragraph or even a semester course. It involves a life—the example of a life of a teacher committed to freedom, integrity, justice, good will, peace and righteousness. It is more by our example than by our words that young men and women are enabled to become what they are meant to be—kind, honest, upright, wise and committed to the truth. Excellence in education, research and service reflects the quality of our efforts. When all else is forgotten by a former student from his or her experience at our universities, colleges and schools of veterinary medicine, there remains the refreshing residue of the impact of one person on another. The example, the wisdom, the inspiration and the experience of maturity impacts receptive, formative youth. As we teach our students we must remember that if we are not here to help other people, there is probably not a good reason for us to be here at all.

Leo K. Bustad: A Photo Essay

Counter Clockwise from Top Left: Leo's fondness for animals started early in life. Here, in about 1931, he spends time with his pet dog, Rusty, in Stanwood, Washington.

Leo and his soon-to-be wife, Signe, in front of her sorority, Chi Omega, on their graduation day, June 9, 1941, from Washington State University.

The Bustad family in 1954 lighting advent candles: (left to right) Leo K., Becky, Leo B. (Buzz), Karen, and Signe.

Leo and his wife, Signe, after his release from prison camp in the summer of 1945.

Above: Although small and shaggy, Bridget was an indispensable member of the Bustad family for more than a decade. Trainer Terry Ryan (left) trained her as a hearing dog for Leo's wife Signe (right) in 1981. Bridget served faithfully until her death in 1994.

Above: As a speaker in high demand, the peripatetic Leo Bustad has given addresses around the world, including many graduation talks at high schools, community colleges and universities.

Below: With years of hard work, Leo helped bring to fruition new facilities for the College of Veterinary Medicine at Washington State University. In recognition of his efforts, the governor and Board of Regents named the first building after him in 1985.

Above: Congratulating Nobel Laureate Konrad Lorenz at a conference in Vienna following Leo's accolades to Dr. Lorenz on behalf of the English-speaking world. The International Symposium on the Human-Pet Relationship, October 1983, honored Lorenz on his 80th birthday.

Below: At the age of 16, Charlie still loved to chase cars, especially Rabbits (with a little help from Leo).

Below: Ties can be practical, Leo proves. He is known for this particular tie, one with a zipper in front, where he can store speech notes...or dessert.
Photo by Henry Moore, 1990.

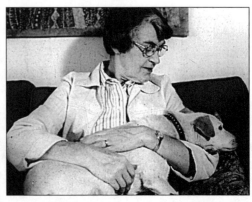

Above: When Leo traveled out of town, he left Signe with "Great Reluctance," their pet dog (also known as Charlie). Photo by Ken Porter, 1978.

Above: Leo has been known for his fondness for pigs—even at the table. *Photo by WSU Biomedical Communications, 1983.*

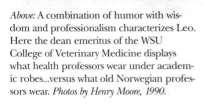

Above: A combination of humor with wisdom and professionalism characterizes Leo. Here the dean emeritus of the WSU College of Veterinary Medicine displays what health professors wear under academic robes...versus what old Norwegian professors wear. *Photos by Henry Moore, 1990.*

At Right: Leo engages in his favorite hobby, birding, whenever and wherever possible.

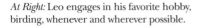

Bridget's Last Ride

*E*arly Monday morning, February 21, 1994, my wife Signe and her hearing dog, Bridget, and I drove to the Washington State University Veterinary Clinic to meet with Dr. Steve Marks, Bridget's compassionate clinician. He was treating her as her health deteriorated, and was as concerned about her condition as if she were his own dog. On the previous Thursday, X-rays had disclosed the cancer in her lungs (which proved to have metastasized to her kidneys, muscles and other tissues). On Friday, we decided to give her a blood transfusion so she could enjoy some quality time on the weekend, which she did. We took her for very short walks, and also on a ride to my office, which she had always enjoyed. By Sunday night, however, Signe was convinced that Bridget had no future, and didn't want to suffer more. So Monday morning was Bridget's last ride, and she departed this world peacefully in Signe's arms as we all shed tears.

The first Sunday after Bridget's death, the following announcement appeared in the church bulletin: "Flowers today are in loving memory of Bridget, Signe Bustad's hearing dog for over twelve years. She had a special talent for children's sermons here and in other churches and was especially fond of children's parties, where much food was spilled. She enjoyed Mature Lutherans potlucks, where food was surreptitiously given her. Bridget was also an active member of the Women's Quilting Group."

This requires some interpretation. Mature Lutherans is a monthly luncheon group that meets at our church in which members seek to outdo one another in the delectability of their food contributions. Every Monday afternoon, Bridget routinely accompanied Signe to a women's group that makes quilts for Lutheran World Relief. When the quilt pieces were arranged on the floor to the quilters' satisfaction, Bridget would come and lie on them. So the women made a special quilt for her, which she loved to sleep on there and at home.

The pastor of the church devoted almost half of his sermon to pay tribute to Bridget. He regarded her as a model for all of us whose assignment is loyal servanthood to be servants to all in need.

Bridget was born in October 1977. We met her at Linda Wilson's home on Thanksgiving of 1979, shortly before Signe's dog, Charlie (Great Reluctance), died. Linda was moving and couldn't bring her dog and was looking for a home for her. I suggested Signe should bring the dog home for a couple of weeks, which she did. A year and one half later we experienced tragedy when Signe lost her hearing. Signe didn't think it was fair to bring in a hearing dog when Bridget was just getting socialized, nor would she part with Bridget for the months it would take to train her as a hearing dog. So Terry Ryan, our friend and associate and expert dog trainer, came to our rescue and offered to train Bridget in our home. She did this under the guidance of Sheila O'Brien of the Hearing Ear Dog Program of West Boylston, Massachusetts (now the National Education of Assistance Dog Services [NEADS]). Bridget was certified as a hearing dog after almost a year of training. A strong bond formed between Bridget and Signe, and Bridget served her well.

Bridget was a great crowd pleaser. People were impressed with her and applauded when she completed a demonstration. And Bridget would bark and jump happily about, because clapping was her signal for playtime. She was a smart little dog. When the phone rang four times during one dinner hour, she alerted Signe only to have Signe answer it and hand it over to me. On the fifth call, she went right to me! During the last year, Bridget also became deaf, but if she saw us talking on the phone she'd jump on Signe as though she had alerted us to its ring.

She was a lovable little dog, she brought us much joy, and we miss her sorely. Hearing dogs are not forever, but their loving memory is.

Concern For Children

The subject of curriculum has been a long-term interest of mine since I have devoted much of my life to the field of education. I have a special concern regarding the education of children. I often tell people things I would do if I became dictator. One of the first things I'd do is to attract the most capable people into elementary education, pay them well and limit their class size to 10 or 12. Kindergarten, first and second grade are a special delight to teach (followed by elderly people who attend elderhostels, many of whom still retain the over-enthusiasm of youth). This interest in children's education is reflected in several of my writings, e.g., the presentation by myself and Linda Hines at an international conference in 1980 sponsored by the British Small Animal Veterinary Association in London (Bustad and Hines, 1980). Some extracts of this presentation are included in this article.

The people-companion animal bond can and should be an integral part of education from a child's earliest classroom experiences, through the university years and throughout life. At all levels, any curriculum which addresses human-animal relationships should develop particular qualities of mind and character rather than limited, time-dated skills. The most important of these qualities are:

- Sensitivity, which includes appreciation of, and delight in, animals,
- understanding, which becomes more complex as the learner matures and is instructed in the various sciences,
- involvement of the learner in the human-animal bond, and
- responsibility in human-animal relationships for the benefit of people and society.

In the earliest years, a child's sensitivity to the world of animals is developed through reading and storytelling. The child delights in fantasy-world animals, and through that fantasy world becomes aware of certain values, principles and moral truths. Since the various animals are anthropomorphized, the child confronts qualities which are both animal and human. Fortunate is the child whose early years have contained an introduction to Gene Zion's *Harry the Dirty Dog*; to the rabbit, cat and walrus in Lewis Carroll's *Alice in Wonderland*; to Mole and his companions in Kenneth Grahame's *The Wind in the Willows*; to C.S. Lewis' lion and mythic characters of *The Chronicles of Narnia*; to E.B. White's remarkable Stuart Little the mouse, Charlotte the spider and Wilbur the pig; and to

Rudyard Kipling's Rikki-tikki-tavi in *The Jungle Books*.

Children can also become aware of the impact of the animal world on the human being through hearing their native folklore. Listening to the tales of the Indian people of Eastern Washington, Native American children grew up learning of Owl Woman, Coyote and Salmon and others, and how their actions, moral and amoral, influenced the human-like community. As explained by Humishumi, or Mourning Dove: "Vividly we recall old *S'whist-kane* (Lost-Head), also known as Old Narciss, and how, in the course of a narrative, he would jump up and mimic his characters, speaking or singing in a strong or weak voice, just as the Animal Persons were supposed to have done. And he would dance around the fire in the tulemat-covered lodge until the pines rang with the gleeful shouts of the smallest listeners. We thought of this as all fun and play, hardly aware that the tale-telling and impersonations were a part of our primitive education." (Hines, 1976)

This process of making children sensitive not only to the animal world, but to the moral consequences of the actions of animals (and by implication, similar human actions) is an important first step in establishing the animal-human bond. A child's sensitivity to, and appreciation for, animals is further broadened through fictional accounts of animals in a more realistic setting. Lassie the dog, Flicka the horse, Miss Piggy of the Muppets, Snoopy the dog and other memorable animal heroes and heroines interact with "real" children in novels and on television.

In addition to learning about animals and the human-animal bond through reading and storytelling, the curriculum for children can build upon the sensitivity, appreciation and delight being awakened in fiction and provide a sound understanding of the world of real animals. Many classrooms contain pets for the children's observation, such as cages of gerbils or guinea pigs or tanks of fish. This is important because increasing numbers of children, especially in urban settings, are growing up without the animal contact that characterized a more rural society. According to the 1970 U.S. Census of Population and Housing, since 1960 the percentage of increase in multi-family units (which usually ban animals) was five times greater than the increase in single-family units.

Schools can fill this gap by teaching about the environment and characteristics of real, specific animals. Children can read books on the life of a gerbil, the care of a dog, or the life cycle of the frog. As they begin to differentiate between the anthropomorphized animals of their fantasy and the real animals that surround them, their understanding of what these real animals do and mean to human existence begins.

The understanding and natural curiosity of children can be broadened through actual involvement with real animals. Through sharing and through experiencing contact with real animals, the students reinforce the facts taught about animals in their classroom. By routinely caring for animals in the classroom or the home, children learn the rudiments of responsibility of people for animals, and also the bond from animal to human that comes from the quiet delight of holding a "warm furry." It is important at this early stage that the children have actual hands-on experience with several animal species (a variety of warm fuzzies). It is also important to expose them early to the importance of wild animals to society and the importance of not trying to make them into pets.

During these early years, the attitudes of teachers and parents are critical in shaping the quality of the human-animal bond developing in the children. The teacher's attitude toward non-human life is often imprinted on the children in the classroom. This highlights the importance of incorporating course work which focuses on the psychological and physiological aspects of the companion animal-human bond in the teacher education curricula. This is a critical dimension if we are ever going to properly inculcate into our young a healthy respect, care, concern, and appreciation for, as well as knowledge about, animals.

In order to engender respect and responsibility for the well-being of animals, we developed a manual entitled *Learning and Living Together: Building the Human-Animal Bond* (Vaughan et al., 1986), which includes sections on teaching methodologies, on how to start a pet education program, and on how to train volunteers and instructors. Over one half of the manual is devoted to lesson plans for preschool through the sixth grade and includes the following subjects:

- Getting acquainted with pets
- Little critters as pets
- Cats as pets
- Dogs as pets
- When your best friend is gone: pet loss and bereavement
- Dog bite prevention

Hill's Pet Nutrition, Inc. made the volume available to veterinarians and associates who "adopted" a classroom and used the handbook.

Our mission is to instill in children an enduring appreciation of the value and wonder of animals and our relationship with them. There is a profound need in people for this relationship, and there is no substitute for it. Animals play an important role in the development of the mind, especially language skills. Animals are important in shaping personality and social consciousness.

In regard to our place on planet Earth my views, like those of other authors, are consistent with those of many Native Americans. I live in the Palouse of eastern Washington and western Idaho—land of Chief Joseph and the Nez Perce. These ancient Native Americans, who refer to themselves as "The Real People," have a profound comprehension of reality and truth. The word "religion" is not in their vocabulary, for everything has sacred significance. Nature is Mother Earth; the minerals within her, the vegetation that springs from her, and the animals that roam over her are all sacred. They, along with other groups of enlightened inhabitants of our planet, believe that animals, plants, and the earth are like vital parts of our body—if these parts are compromised, we seriously harm ourselves. To remain healthy, we must maintain a respectful relationship with all the elements of our environment. A strong people-animal-environment bond is crucial to a healthy community, worldwide.

It is our hope that one person can make a difference, that through the information presented by volunteer instructors, children will develop a true reverence for all of life and accept the charge of responsibility for animals. We believe it is in learning to care for our fellow creatures that we express our finest qualities. Milan Kundera (1984), a contemporary Czechoslovakian writer living in France, has stated:

> True human goodness, in all its purity and freedom, can come to the
> fore only when its recipient has no power. Mankind's true moral test, its
> fundamental test (which lies deeply buried from view), consists of its atti-
> tude towards those who are at its mercy: animals.

We wish all who are involved in teaching our most precious resource—children—success in improving the lives of people and animals—and the environment we share.

Holocausts

On the night of November 9, a very somber ceremony is held in many places in the world. The people who gather wish to remind the world that just after midnight, November 9, 1938, something very terrible happened. It was Krystallnacht—"the night of the broken glass" or "crystal night." It marked the first large-scale violence against the Jews of Austria and Germany. That night the Nazis smashed the windows of Jewish-owned businesses, fire-bombed synagogues, murdered many Jews and arrested thousands. It was a night of horror. It marked the beginning of the German holocaust which resulted in 7 million deaths (5 million Jews and 2 million Gypsies, Poles and others). This was one of the largest mass killings in history, and certainly the most efficient. And it happened in a country considered to be one of the most advanced—rich in culture, music, literature and religion.

Sybil von Sell Niemoeller, widow of Martin Niemoeller who was a U-boat captain in World War I and a pastor and leader in the Nazi-era (World War II) Confessing Church that opposed Adolph Hitler, stated in a talk at Susquehanna University on November 19, 1988:

> *...in essence the Nazi said to the Jews, "You shall not live as Jews among us." Later Hitler added to that "You shall not live among us," and finally "You shall not live."*

Mrs. Niemoeller said her husband used to ask German audiences, "While all this was happening, where were we? Where were you? Where was I?" And to his Jewish audiences he said, "I did so little; please forgive me."

This serves to introduce the soul-searching subject of holocausts.

In my last days as a prisoner of war in Germany during World War II, a survivor of a concentration camp joined us. In my mind's eye, I can see him today as I did that day 43 years ago, and it haunts me still. "Walking dead" describes what I saw—an emaciated person with sunken, dazed eyes. What he had actually experienced came to me much later. The horrible nature and extent of this crime against humanity—this devastation of entire cultures and peoples— is absolutely overwhelming.

I stated it haunts me still. Within the last month I awoke from a deep sleep in terror because I was dreaming that I was on the third tier of a gas chamber and I began smelling cyanide. I should also tell you that awakening in terror is not an uncommon occurrence in my life since I suffer, among other things,

---

This talk was given as an Armistice Day address to ROTC students in November 1988.

from what has been diagnosed as post-traumatic stress disorder (PTSD).

For a very long time I have believed that the reality and horror of genocide should be taught in the curriculum. We must, as teachers, teach what we know and remember; no one should be allowed to forget holocausts that have occurred for eons of years and that reached mammoth proportions in my generation. I was motivated to organize a course entitled "Reverence for Life" in the late 1970s, and the writings of two people especially convinced me to do this.

The first was Nobel Laureate Elie Wiesel, who wrote: "One of the worst moments in life was not during the war, but after. I discovered that during the war the killers, most of them, had college degrees. The entire scientific genius of nations was put to use to produce death. The indifference of the world hurt me very much and still does." Wiesel went on to say that "knowledge without ethical dimensions turns against human beings, turns against humanity."

The second writer, who was a school principal, is nameless, but in a speech Leo Buscaglia credited the words to Haim Ginott's (1972) last book. Ginott had received this poignant statement from this principal:

> My eyes saw what no person should witness:
> Gas chambers built by learned engineers.
> Children poisoned by educated physicians.
> Infants killed by trained nurses.
> Women and babies shot by high school and college graduates.
> So I am suspicious of education.
> My request is: Help your students to be human.
> Your efforts must never produce learned monsters, skilled psychopaths,
>   or educated Eichmanns.

The German holocaust of the 1930s and 1940s receives the most emphasis in my discussion. One of the reasons is that it is the best documented, and more than 200 books have appeared that address the subject. But we must not forget that holocausts have occurred for a long time, and we are still plagued with them in our time. We must not forget the holocausts involving Afghanistanis, Cambodians, Eritreans, Kurds, Tibetans, Tigreans, Russians (especially peasants; upwards of 20 million), Mesquite Indians, and others including many tribes in Africa.

It seems, as my associate and former student Olin Balch said, that the model for Hitler was the successful Turkish genocide against the Armenians in their country prior to World War I. It was considered successful for the following two reasons: (1) It resulted in reduction of the Armenian population from perhaps 1,800,000 to 32,500 at the present time, and (2) there was minimal world condemnation and interference at the time of the genocide. Reading world history demonstrates that genocides such as this are always the result of aberrant political behavior promoted by madmen, and unrestrained nationalism, racism, or religious fanaticism. Genocide is also used as a political tool to consolidate power as leaders convince their people that the target populations are evil, less than human and enemies of the state.

The complicity of health-care providers in the German holocaust is appalling. Robert Conot's *Justice at Nuremberg* (1973) has a section entitled "The

Perversion of German Medicine" which is illuminating. The "final solution" for the Jewish race allowed an activity that involved the employment of human beings for medical experiments and acute anthropological studies (skeletonization). Research mimicking high altitude flights, survival in icy water, and simulated battlefield infections stuffed with gangrene cultures produced few survivors. One of the most appalling statements was: "In early May of 1943, Gebhardt, as the principal speaker before the Congress of Reich Physicians, proudly provided explicit details of the result of these human experiments. Virtually everyone of note in German medicine was there. A number of professors of medicine at various universities led a discussion afterward, and not one of them issued a word of criticism." From this we conclude that medical education and the medical system do not necessarily promote reverence and respect for life. Given a political system that will relegate a group of people to "pariah" status resulting in broad societal efforts of "demonization" and dehumanization, the medical establishment will fully cooperate. This further convinced us that sanctity of life must be taught.

One of the most impressive discriminants of the terrible mental anguish associated with holocausts appears in William Styron's *Sophie's Choice* (1979). Sophie appears before an inebriated physician who says to her, "You may keep one of your children." Shocked in disbelief, Sophie appears stunned, so the physician repeats his statement:

> "You may keep one of your children," he repeated. "The other one will have to go. Which one will you keep?"
>
> "You mean, I have to choose?"
>
> "You're a Polack, not a Yid. That gives you a privilege—a choice."
>
> Her thought processes dwindled, ceased. Then she felt her legs crumple. "I can't choose! I can't choose!" She began to scream. Oh, how she recalled her own screams! Tormented angels never screeched so loudly above hell's pandemonium. *"Ich kann nicht wählen!"* she screamed.
>
> The doctor was aware of unwanted attention. "Shut up!" he ordered. "Hurry now and choose...or I'll send them both over there. Quick!"
>
> She could not believe any of this. She could not believe that she was now kneeling on the hurtful, abrading concrete, drawing her children toward her so smotheringly tight that she felt that their flesh might be engrafted to hers even through layers of clothes. Her disbelief was total, deranged....
>
> "Don't make me choose," she heard herself plead in a whisper, "I can't choose."
>
> "Send them both over there, then," the doctor said to the aide, *"nach links."*
>
> "Mama!" She heard Eva's thin but soaring cry at the instant that she thrust the child away from her and rose from the concrete with a clumsy stumbling motion. "Take the baby!" she called out. "Take my little girl!"
>
> At this point the aide—with a careful gentleness that Sophie would try without success to forget—tugged at Eva's hand and led her away into the waiting legion of the damned. She would forever retain a dim

impression that the child had continued to look back, beseeching. But because she was almost completely blinded by salty, thick, copious tears she was spared whatever expression Eva wore, and she was always grateful for that. For in the bleakest honesty of her heart she knew that she would never have been able to tolerate it, driven nearly mad as she was by her last glimpse of that vanishing small form.

I want my students to realize that Sophie or anyone going through such an experience will suffer forever the agony of the moment. It is the ultimate of tragedy, and this tragedy was repeated countless times in real life during the German holocaust and others.

One of the most impressive insights into the adversity and dehumanizing aspects of the concentration camps of Auschwitz and Dachau is written in *Man's Search for Meaning* (1963) by Dr. Viktor Frankl, a psychiatrist. I recommend this book to many people and most especially students in my class "Reverence for Life." One of the subjects I discuss in this course is genocide, and I usually read some choice portions that exhibit Dr. Frankl's wisdom, courage and humanness. One of my favorites is on hope at a very depressing time in his sixth year of World War II. It was an evening of a day of fasting. The prisoners were lying in the huts—many were on the verge of despair, and to make the situation worse the lights went out. The wise senior block warden recognized the depressed state of the prisoners and gave a brief analysis of the recent deaths of many of their comrades. He felt the real reason for the deaths was the giving up of hope and suggested that there should be some way of preventing such deaths. The warden then fingered Dr. Frankl for advice. Dr. Frankl told his comrades things could be worse, that few had irreplaceable losses. He then said:

> Whoever was still alive had reason for hope. Health, family, happiness, professional abilities, fortune, position in society—these were things that could be achieved again or restored. After all, we still had all our bones intact. Whatever we had gone through could still be an asset to us in the future.

Dr. Frankl then quoted from Nietzche: "That which does not kill me makes me stronger."

He then addressed their future. Although he felt his own chances were only about one in 20, he had no intention of losing hope and giving up, for often unexpected things happen. He also recalled for his comrades the past: "all its joys, and how its light shone even in the present darkness." He quoted a poet, "What you have experienced, no power on earth can take from you."

He then spoke to his comrades of the many opportunities they still had to give life meaning and told them that "human life, under any circumstance, never ceased to have a meaning, and that this infinite meaning of life includes suffering and dying, privation and death." Dr. Frankl entreated those who were suffering so terribly to not lose hope; that "the hopelessness of our struggle did not detract from its dignity and meaning."

Dr. Frankl did not want them to die for nothing! And then he closed his "homily" with these words:

The purpose of my words was to find a full meaning in our life, then and there, in that hut and in that practically hopeless situation. I saw that my efforts had been successful. When the electric bulb flared up again, I saw the miserable figures of my friends limping toward me to thank me with tears in their eyes. But I have to confess here that only too rarely had I the inner strength to make contact with my companions in suffering and that I must have missed many opportunities for doing so.

Unfortunately we can all make the same confession.

On Touch and Gentling

*A*mong my fondest recollections of my youth regarding nurture was the tender touch of my parents. When I was ill, my father, who was not given to displaying emotion, would always come to my sickbed and stroke my forehead and cheeks. My mother and grandmother, who displayed more emotion and were more demonstrative, often touched and stroked me. My favorite aunt, Kari (my father's sister), was a great nurturer too. She gave me a lot of strokes. I have only happy memories of this compassionate person and my nurturing parents and grandmother.

With my children, I took a page out of the life of these dear, nurturing people. When any of our children were ill or otherwise distressed, I would kiss and tenderly stroke their foreheads and cheeks with my hand. In doing so, I comforted them and also determined if they were feverish. On one occasion when our son, then in the first grade, was very ill for several days, a gift of a carefully selected kitten seemed to alleviate all symptoms and he was back in school the following day.

From my parents I learned the importance of touch especially for gentling animals. We were instructed to pet and speak kindly to the animals: cats, cows, dogs, goats, horses and pigs. For the production animals, my father said they'd do better if they were gently cared for; later I learned from many studies that my father was right. A review of some of the observations by a number of people working with animals is enlightening:

- A number of people have observed that petting an animal can reduce blood pressure, heart rate, and rate and depth of breathing in the animal. Petting an animal can reduce blood pressure and contribute to relaxation and longevity in the person, as well.
- Immunity can be enhanced by the handling and gentling of very young animals. It was found that handling young mice daily for 21 days increased their antibody response.
- Recent studies in the handling of infant rats for brief periods resulted in changes of cellular components in certain areas of the central nervous system.
- In an older study, it was reported that rats gently handled from ages 21 to 60 days were superior in performing discrimination tasks and also gained more weight.

First published in slightly longer form in *The Caring Communique* vol. 2 no. 1, 1995.

- In studies at Virginia Polytech, chickens were socialized by using a gentle approach to them, stroking their backs and speaking to them. The chickens were also trained to perch on the caretaker's hands, which seemed to have a calming effect on the birds. The socialized birds produced more antibodies, had more blood protein, gained more weight, and were more resistant to certain disease organisms.
- My friend Dr. Albright of Purdue University recalled some studies in England and the U.S. that showed significant relationships between personality characteristics of herdsmen and milk production in cows. A survey of 50 one-man dairy herds of 50 to 80 cows showed 11 percent more milk production and greater willingness of the cows to enter the milking area in cows handled by herdsmen classified as confident introverts, than in herdsmen classified as confident extroverts.
- Australian work on pigs showed that brief exposure of 11-week-old pigs (three times a week for two minutes a day) for a total of 11 weeks to either a pleasant or unpleasant experience with a person had a dramatic effect on conception rate (87 percent versus 33 percent). Earlier sexual maturity, better feed utilization, and increased weight gain were also observed in the gentled group.

Twenty years ago, my friends Sam and Elizabeth Corson at Ohio State University introduced me to a book on touching by Ashley Montagu (Montagu, 1971, 1978). The opening sentence in this fascinating book is, "The skin like a cloak covers us all over, the oldest and most sensitive of our organs, our first medium of communication and our most efficient of all protectors!" Montague also quoted from Lionell Taylor's 1921 book *The Stages of Life*. "The greatest sense in our body is our touch sense."

Until recently the age-old custom of laying on of hands was not understood. Continuous stimulation begins before birth and the nerve fibers for touch are among the earliest to fully develop. It is interesting to note that the Corsons reminded us that the earlier a function develops, the more fundamental it is likely to be. Touch sensation, they deduce, represents significant input essential for optimal physical, emotional and mental health.

During my lifetime with the development of "high tech" in medical care, there was a decline in touch as an integral part of healing. It appears there's been a resurgence of interest in the importance of touch in the healing process. The importance of touch in human-animal interactions has been emphasized and expanded on in the past two decades.

Infant rats, after even short-term separation from their mothers, show adverse effects including alteration in the activity of an enzyme which is important in protein synthesis and the secretion of corticosterone as well as growth hormone. Activity can be restored by reuniting the mother and offspring (or by licking action on the rats). Intermittent, heavy brush stroking effectively reverses or prevents all the changes associated with maternal deprivation. In the absence of touch, of social contact, terminal apathy may be the infant's fate. It has been reported that very small, pre-term neonates when given tactile stimulation gain more weight per day, spend more time awake and active, and exhibit other favorable responses.

The positive effects of nurturing on the one who is nurturing, as well as the nurtured, contributes especially to the health and well-being of the young, the elderly and/or people with disabilities—and contributes to the survival of the species. It appears that nurturing others decreases aggression; this beneficial effect may be greatest in the male population.

In closing, I remind you that although touch is silent, it is the most remarkable channel of communication and is exceedingly powerful. If you love someone, you can touch that person even if you are not with them. Touch can bless, comfort, welcome, honor, respect, persuade, influence, inflame. So use it wisely, respectfully and compassionately, for tender touching can be great therapy!

Prison Programs Involving Animals

This paper needs little introduction. I have been interested in animals in institutions since my youth. As a former prisoner of war, I have some comprehension of what it's like to be incarcerated—to have no "key to the compound." I believe careful introduction and monitoring of animals into many prisons can have remarkable effects on the prisoners, animals and eventual recipients of the animals they train. The results to date substantiate our beliefs in this regard.

Introducing animals into prisons may be the most impressive and significant of all human-animal interactions. Because people are by nature nurturers, without suitable nurturing objects or appropriate nurture they cannot be expected to function satisfactorily in society. My observations and readings over the last 50 years have led me to this conclusion. One book that impressed me was Dr. Boris Levinson's *Pets and Human Development* (1972). He wrote a chapter devoted to pets in correctional institutions and referred to many programs that have been conducted throughout the years. He concluded that pets are perhaps more needed in correctional institutions than in any other type of institution.

In 1936 and 1937, while in the Future Farmers of America Club and a member of various judging teams, I visited several institutions, including mental hospitals and reformatories, where many fine animals were kept. It appeared that the animals were treated very well and were important to the institutionalized residents. Also at this time I recall being impressed by Lord Byron's poem, "The Prisoner of Chillon." I was most impressed with these verses:

> With spiders I had friendship made,
> And watched them in their sullen trade
> Had seen the mice by moonlight play,
> And why should I feel less than they?
> We were all inmates of one place,
> And I, the monarch of each race,
> Had power to kill—yet, strange to tell!
> In quiet we had learned to dwell.

During 1944 and 1945 I was incarcerated as a prisoner of war; for the first time in my life I was separated from animals. In my reading after the war, I came to realize that for centuries herds and flocks were kept on prison farms as well as other institutions to provide food and fiber as well as employment opportunities for the inmates. Yet during my adult lifetime I have witnessed an unfortunate reduction in herds and flocks and, in many cases, an abolition of any animal contact by people in institutions. Fortunately, there is now a rekindling of interest, and animals are being introduced into institutions not only in our country, but throughout the world.

In the 1970s I became very involved in a community-university program involving volunteers and animals in a variety of situations, i.e., working with children, the elderly, and people with disabilities. With Linda Hines (now the Executive Director of the Delta Society), we formed the People-Pet Partnership, and during this time we met Kathy Quinn (now Sister Pauline). Kathy had been incarcerated 35 times in 14 different institutions for a total of about six years, beginning at the age of 13. On several occasions we discussed the great benefits that might accrue to an inmate if animal association was provided.

In 1980, Kathy, who had extensive experience with dogs, borrowed a wheelchair and trained one of her dogs to assist her while in the wheelchair. Because of her success, she proposed an interesting plan. She had met a person with a developmental disability who was interested in a companion animal. She proposed we go to the Purdy Correction Center for Women (now the Washington State Correction Center for Women), a maximum security prison, and, with excellent trainers, assist selected inmates in training animals to help people with disabilities. I also suggested that we have prisoners give obedience training to selected dogs from the Tacoma-Pierce County Humane Society so that they would be better candidates for adoption. Both Linda Hines and I approved the idea and assisted Kathy. The plan was eventually implemented as a pilot study in 1981 and was the first of its type devoted to prisoner training of dogs to help people with disabilities.

In 1983-84, as president of the Delta Society, I established an international task force on animals in prisons. Members of the team were people involved in such programs or who had great interest in these programs and who, because of their influential positions and/or their expertise in corrections, could aid in implementing such programs in North America, Australia, Africa, Europe, and Asia.

The following are overviews of selected animal programs, many of them discussed at the 1989 International Conference in Monaco on the Relationship Between Humans and Animals and at later conferences. The information was obtained largely from personal communications, by telephone or letter, from the people involved in designing and administering these programs. In preparing the second edition of this book I requested up-dates from all the programs mentioned in the first edition, and many of them responded with helpful information, which is included here. Descriptions of those that did not respond have been left unchanged or, in a few cases, eliminated. Some prison animal projects have been terminated, usually for lack of funds, and others have been modified; new programs are implemented from time to time, and several are included here. All these programs illustrate the benefits that can accrue to prisoners (helping them to be better people and to function in law-abiding ways), to animals (often saving their lives), and to the community at large (providing needed service dogs and companion animals, plus services such as training and grooming). I am always eager to learn about new prison animal programs or developments in existing ones, and I would appreciate hearing from readers who have additional information in this field.

Oakwood Forensic Center
Lima, Ohio—David R. Lee

This program was initiated by David Lee in 1975. I believe it was the first structured program involving animals with prisoners in a maximum security institution. A year-long study here compared two wards, identical except that only one had pets. The ward with pets required half the medication of the other, had less violence and no suicide attempts, while the ward without pets had at least eight suicide attempts. After 21 years this program still serves low functioning mentally ill patients, those with mental retardation, depression or suicidal tendencies. The animals reside full-time either in the correctional facility units (e.g., birds, hamsters, and fish) or in a large yard where deer, goats, ducks, and sheep are kept. The inmates have worked with the local game warden, treating injured wildlife, and have rehabilitated deer, pheasants, peacocks, pygmy goats, geese, and ducks that would otherwise have been destroyed. In 1994 a llama was introduced and became a "primary therapist" for patients with extreme problems. In 1996 inmates began training pups for the Pilot Dog program. The pups are trained here for one year and then transferred to Columbus, Ohio, for advanced training.

The apparent success of Larry the Llama is heartening. He was a gift from David Lee, who had no doubt extended loving nurture to this pet.

Ohio Correctional System/Pilot Dog Program
Columbus, Ohio—Jay Gray

As of 1996, 49 prisoners in 13 Ohio penitentiaries were engaged in raising pups for Pilot Dogs Inc., a Columbus, Ohio, organization that provides free guide dogs for people who are blind. The prisoners nurture the dogs and give them obedience training for about a year. The dogs get 24-hour-a-day human contact, which is ideal for training guide dogs. The dogs are then sent to Columbus for several months of advanced training. Jay Gray, executive director of Pilot Dogs, started the program in 1993. In the first three years, about 90 dogs were trained by prisoners. Ordinarily about 60% of the puppies trained in foster homes graduate to become guide dogs, but the success rate for Ohio's prison-reared dogs is 80%.

Prison-Pet Partnership Program (PPPP)
Washington State Correction Center for Women
Gig Harbor, Washington—Jeanne Hampl

In the early 1980s, a program providing custom training of dogs to fill special needs of people with disabilities was begun in this maximum security prison by Kathy Quinn (now Sister Pauline) and associates Dawn Jecs and Marsha Henkle, Linda Hines and myself, and Linda McCuistion. The program also offered community college instruction for prisoners in grooming, canine husbandry and behavior, and obedience training for dogs from the humane society shelter, thus improving chances for satisfactory adoption of the dogs. After some reorganization the program appears to be in full operation, training dogs and giving participating inmates a sense of purpose, a more wholesome outlook and positive skills. One of the most exciting developments is that a few of the prison-trained dogs can detect the onset of seizures in people even before they become manifest.

Liberty Dog Program, Green Bay Correctional Institution
Green Bay, Wisconsin—Sister Pauline Quinn and Daniel R. Bertrand

This new (1996) program is based on community involvement. A kennel is being built in a former storage area with the help of volunteers who contribute skilled and unskilled labor as well as construction materials. A pet food manufacturer has agreed to supply the animals' food, and another firm is donating leashes and grooming equipment. Volunteers for the program include Dr. Neil Rechsteiner, a local veterinarian, and June Ashford, head trainer at a local pet care center. Under her direction and with the help of other volunteer trainers, inmates will socialize and train service dogs for people with disabilities. Participating inmates will learn dog training, grooming and handling skills that may help them find employment after their release. Warden Bertrand believes that the program will also help them learn positive ways of interacting with other people and improve their attitudes toward those with disabilities.

Animal Program at the District of Columbia Correctional Facility
Lorton, Virginia—Earl Strimple

The People-Animals-Love (PAL) program at the Lorton Prison in Washington, D.C., was founded in 1982 by veterinarian Earl Strimple (a leading authority on animals and prisoners) and Sophie Engelhard, who contributed a great deal to the prison program, with help from volunteer associates. It offers placement of animals (cats, birds, fish and rabbits) and has established a club where animal needs are discussed and animal care instruction is given. A vocational course in animal health technology has been developed with assistance from the personnel of the National Institutes of Health and the Uniformed Services University of the Health Sciences. Upon release, many graduates of this course have found jobs in laboratory animal facilities.

IMPACT Program (Inmates Providing Animal Care and Training)
Gainesville Work Camp
Gainesville, Florida—Tom Lane

Since this program was started in 1991, at least 18 dogs have been trained as guide dogs for people who are blind. Dr. Lane works with the Southeastern Guide Dog Association to obtain puppies, each of which is assigned to a selected inmate for 9-12 months training. At the end of this period, the dogs are returned to the Association to be matched with a person needing a guide dog. During their training period, the dogs are also taken to visit nursing homes and child care facilities. Inmates can enroll in a vocational training program, with classes taught by volunteers including veterinary technicians, veterinary students, and dog trainers.

Colorado Wild Horse Inmate Program, Four Mile Correctional Facility
Canon City, Colorado—Tony Bainbridge

This program was initiated in 1986 by veterinarian Dr. Ron Zaidlicz at the Fremont Correctional Facility. In cooperation with the Bureau of Land Management and the American Humane Association, it offered a rehabilitation program through which inmates were taught horsemanship, animal husbandry, farrier and veterinary technician skills. Inmates were also involved in the training of wild horses to improve the chances of successful adoptions. Dr. Zaidlicz left the program in 1989, but it has continued in a different form under the direction of Tony Bainbridge, who has been with the program since its inception. An average of 25 inmates are enrolled in an Equine Management course designed to prepare them for employment upon their release. (Until 1995 they could receive college credit for the course.) The Bureau of Land Management's participation ceased in 1993, due to federal budget cuts, and the program is now self-sufficient. The facility is the largest in the world for training wild horses, and by 1996 had trained over 2,700 inmates and about 4,000 horses.

The program also offers training of privately owned horses that have been deemed untrainable by other training operations. There are plans to purchase untrained domestic horses, train them, and offer them for resale to the public. This would give inmates an opportunity to learn different training methods for different types of horses and increase their chances of finding employment in equine-related professions.

Central New Mexico Correctional Facility, Pet Visitation Program
Los Lunas, New Mexico—Molly Evanko

Docents from the zoo and volunteers from the humane society and Wonderful World of Pets made weekly visits to the correctional facility with an assortment of zoo and other animals. Instruction was given regarding the history, needs and personalities of the animals, thus providing an educational and enjoyable experience. Sharon Powell, a former docent and President of Human Animal Partnership, directed the program in 1989.

Texas Department of Corrections Canine Research Unit
Huntsville, Texas—James D. McCrady

The Canine Research Unit was established as a joint program between the Texas Department of Corrections and Baylor College of Medicine in 1963 for the purpose of producing dogs for research and maintaining long-term holding of research animals to benefit the inmates and the animals. The program was later expanded. Since Dr. McCrady is now occupied with an international program, current information may be obtained from the Director of Laboratory Animal Medicine, Baylor College of Medicine, Houston, Texas.

Leader Dog Project, Huron Valley Women's Correctional Facility
Ypsilanti, Michigan—Carol Dyer

This program was established in 1988 to provide disability service agencies with a source of dogs that were socialized and given basic training by the female inmates. After one year at the facility, dogs are sent to the Rochester Leader Dog

School for final training. Kennels and grooming facilities have been constructed. Selected inmates learn training and grooming skills, as well as learning of the needs and accomplishments of people with disabilities. Dogs are taken throughout the prison so that as many inmates as possible have contact with them. This helps in the dogs' socialization and also benefits inmates.

Friends for Folks, Lexington Assessment and Reception Center
Lexington, Oklahoma—Sergeant Jack Cottrell

This program, which was dedicated on July 31, 1990, allows long-term prisoners to train animals from local shelters as companions for single elderly people or as service dogs for people with disabilities. Prisoners are rotated through the program so that as many as possible are involved. In the new High Intensity Training program (HIT), dog owners can have their pets trained in 30 days for a donation of $50.

Correctional Critters, Connecticut Department of Correction
Hartford, Connecticut

The program was introduced in 1992 to reduce tension, develop responsibility among inmates, and improve inmate-staff communication. Each facility initiates a "critter committee" composed of staff and inmates, who work out the rules and procedures for keeping one or more animals. One or two carefully selected dogs are then assigned to each prison. Other "critters" have included fish, hamsters, a parrot, a garter snake, and a hermit crab.

Pet-Grooming Program, Pitchess Detention Center
Castaic, California—Debbie Pieropan

In this program, inmates learn to groom dogs and cats from a county animal shelter, improving the animals' chances of being adopted. For a $10 fee, inmates also groom pets belonging to jail employees; these fees cover the costs involved in grooming the shelter animals. As of August, 1996, an inmate's sentence is reduced by about five days for every 20 days worked in the grooming unit. On completion of 120 hours work, each participating inmate receives an adult education certificate. Several former students have obtained jobs in the pet industry.

Project POOCH, MacLaren School, Oregon Youth Authority
Woodburn, Oregon—Joan Dalton

In 1993, Delta Society and MacLaren School, a juvenile correctional facility for males, initiated Project POOCH (Positive Opportunities - Obvious Change with Hounds). Juvenile offenders adopt dogs from two local humane societies and give the dogs obedience training with the help of their classroom teacher, who is also a dog trainer. The dogs are then adopted by families in the community. The program is funded through donations and private donors, and is an approved vocational program. All the students who have participated have decreased their number of office referrals, and show improved self-esteem, patience, responsibility, and vocational skills. Project POOCH II, now being developed, will add dog grooming, kennel management, and veterinary technician training for long-term residents.

British Columbia Prison Programs Involving Animals
Maple Ridge, British Columbia, Canada—Tom Cadieux

Several facilities in the B.C. Corrections Branch have programs that involve inmates working with animals. The Alouette River Correctional Centre in Maple Ridge has an extensive aquaculture program utilizing offender labor.

The Allco Hatchery is a salmonoid restoration project for the Alouette River system in partnership with Federal and Provincial fisheries agencies. The ARC facility is an applied science center for the development of a pedigreed rainbow trout for fish farmers, in partnership with the University of British Columbia and the Ministry of Agriculture, Food and Fish. The Bell-cor project on Alouette Lake is a net pen rearing site for rainbow trout. In this partnership the Alouette River Correctional Centre works with B.C. Hydro and the Ministry of Environment, Lands and Parks (Fisheries) with the aim of enhancing hydro lakes.

The Stave Lake Correctional Centre in Maple Ridge has a net pen rearing site which is the sole supplier of rainbow trout for many small lakes. This prison also has an animal shelter which cares for and releases wildlife such as eagles, owls, and deer.

The Burnaby Correctional Centre for Women has a pet therapy program, under the direction of Kathy Gibson, in which inmates work with dogs.

Calgary Wildlife Rehabilitation Society
Calgary, Alberta, Canada—Jill Sorenson

Since 1994 this society has worked with two prisons in the United States, involving inmates in wildlife rehabilitation. The inmates provide long-term care for injured wildlife received by Calgary veterinarians from the general public. They also help with a quarterly newsletter and keep wildlife case records, thus learning marketable business skills.

Community Services Aquatic Club, Saughton Prison
Edinburgh, Scotland—Dick McLaine

Long-term prisoners began working in 1978 in cooperation with Stirling University Marine Biology Department rearing fish, chiefly for Third World countries. Through this program, breeding stocks were improved and thousands of fish were sent to developing countries to increase food supplies. Prawn production was developed, and some prisoners also developed an aviary. The edible fish breeding program has been terminated, but prisoners still breed tropical fish, which they exchange for food and equipment. Some raise budgies and cockatiels in their cells. Surplus birds are given to hospitals or to elderly people and children in need.

Pets as Therapy Program (PAT), Adelaide Women's Prison
Northfield, South Australia—Don Verlander and Paul Walsh

In 1988 the Guide Dogs Association of South Australia and Northern Territory Inc., a well-established organization with a long track record, commenced a program to help people who have disabilities or are otherwise disadvantaged. Selected inmates are involved in supervised training of the PAT dogs in special tasks, including socialization of the dogs at nearby nursing homes and special education schools. The program includes visits to hospitals and an annual visit to a camp for Girl Guides with various disabilities. By 1996, over 200 inmate-trained dogs had been placed with individuals and families, including victims of crime, socially isolated individuals, children with cerebral palsy, and people with intellectual disabilities, paraplegia or quadriplegia. A controlled study (Walsh and Merten, 1994) showed increased self-esteem and decreased levels of depression among participating inmates. Some prisoners who had not initially volunteered for the PAT program later asked to be included because of the positive changes they noticed in the participants, such as increased calmness, expressions of happiness, and less aggravation and aggression.

Guide Dog Program, Beechworth Training Prison
Beechworth, Victoria, Australia

Probably the first of its kind in Australia, this program began in 1974 as a cooperative project of the prison and the Royal Guide Dogs Association. Puppies are placed in the care of selected low security prisoners who are responsible for the dogs' kennel hygiene, grooming, feeding and exercising. Special permission has been given for the handlers to take the dogs into the shopping area of Beechworth, to expose them to street and traffic conditions, shops and crowds. The program has continued for over 22 years, and although there has been no controlled scientific evaluation of its results, anecdotal reports have been positive.

The Garth Prison Pet Program
Lancashire, England—Mary Whyham

Garth is a Category B (secure) prison established in 1988 for 512 male offenders, serving sentences from four years to life imprisonment. By 1992, over 70 inmates had birds in their cells. Additionally, the prisoners had built two aviaries and were breeding birds for distribution to elderly and disadvantaged people in the community. Fish tanks with tropical fish were set up in the gymnasium and visiting areas. Inmates were involved in their care and breeding. Pet care classes were held in the evenings in conjunction with the education department. Environmental issues and wildlife knowledge were included. The most distinctive feature of the Garth initiative is the coordinated approach to the pet program, involving several departments in the prison.

In a survey of 156 correctional establishments in the United Kingdom, Mary Whyham received information on 86 prisons, 53 of which had some animal interaction.

Companion Animal Programs, Department of Correctional Services
South Africa—Johannes Odendaal

Companion animal programs were introduced to South African prisons in the mid-1980s. In this system, pets are used as an incentive for good behavior. Prisoners are divided into groups A and B on the basis of their behavior, which is reassessed about every six months. Among other privileges, group A prisoners are allowed to keep pets. They are responsible for taking care of their animals, including buying food for them. Lieutenant-Colonel R.P. van Wyk, Head of the

Pretoria Central Prison, has reported using a bowl of fish to calm down aggressive, destructive, or frustrated prisoners. At Groenpunt Prison, Captain Rika Scribante and Lieutenant Anta Marx have found that the presence of birds, fish, or puppies facilitates therapy.

Introduction of animals into prisons may well result in the most rewarding of all human-animal interactions. The benefits that might accrue include:

1. Providing vocational training and employment. Keeping of herds and flocks at correctional facilities has diminished in recent times, but is still fortunately practiced in the United States, the United Kingdom, Germany, Scandinavia, and probably many other countries. The emphasis in recent times has been on vocational training. Employment opportunities are extensive and include maintaining cattle, swine, sheep, chickens, turkeys, fish, and some laboratory animals for commercial purposes, as well as keeping and training dogs and horses. Vocational training is involved in keeping these animals, and inmates have found employment in these activities following release.

2. Helping people with disabilities as well as animals and the community at large. In the program at the Washington State Correction Center for Women, selected women prisoners give obedience and special training to dogs obtained chiefly from a large humane society. This vocational training program is supervised by excellent trainers and serves as a model for prisons to consider. Many community members benefit by such an activity, as do the inmates who are heroes to the recipients of the dogs they have trained, and of course it also saves many dogs from euthanasia and provides them with good homes.

3. Providing prisoners with a feeling of acceptance and fulfilling a need to nurture. In his 1972 book *Pets and Human Development*, Boris Levinson, a clinical psychologist, stated that the companionship and affection of a pet, and the opportunity to have responsibility for an animal's well-being, promotes emotional growth and self-worth even when other conditions are not necessarily helpful. Also prisoners learn responsibility, cooperation and self-control.

4. Contributing to the well-being of animals. Prisoners have helped animals by: (1) giving obedience or specialized training to selected unwanted animals in animal control centers, thereby making them desirable and useful long-term companions; (2) rehabilitating wildlife and providing a sanctuary for those incapable of being released; and (3) gentling and training "wild" horses to make them acceptable and useful as companion animals. In addition to the benefits from these ongoing programs are the countless untold benefits to animals through the individual, personal interactions they have with the prisoners.

Many, if not all, of the benefits listed above have been demonstrated in prison programs throughout the world. Inmates involved in these programs express their joy at feeling needed and doing something both useful and important. They also feel less anger and stress as they work with, and learn to love and care for, their animal companions. They can see the positive results of their care and nurturing activities. However, there continues to be an urgent need for quantitative studies, including longitudinal ones, on the effects of animal interaction with prisoners. With the detailed information that these studies could provide, more effective programs could be implemented throughout the prison system.

I conclude with a critical responsibility that relates to the well-being of animals in prisons. In any program involving animals in institutions it is incumbent on those responsible to insure the health and well-being of the animals. In my experience, most prisoners who express interest in an animal program are kind and compassionate with the animals. In this regard I am reminded of an incident that occurred on a hot summer day in 1924 in Pike County, Pennsylvania, to Pep, a Labrador retriever who lived in a home next door to Governor and Mrs. Pinchot. In a fit of reckless abandon or due to a territorial incursion, Pep killed Mrs. Pinchot's pet cat. This enraged the Governor who called for an immediate hearing and presided over a trial. Unfortunately, Pep had no legal counsel, and he was sentenced to life imprisonment in the State Penitentiary in Philadelphia. The bewildered warden decided Pep should have a number just like the rest of the inmates; Pep became Canine Convict No. C2559. Pep was lavished with affection and was welcomed in many cells and switched cell mates at will. When the prisoners were building a new penitentiary in another location, every morning Pep eagerly boarded the bus when his number was called. He was one of the first to move into the new quarters and lived happily until he died there in 1930 of old age. Our duty is to strive to insure all animals in prison will be as fortunate as Pep in attracting a large, effective and nurturing support network.

Grief

The death of a child is the ultimate of tragedy, and I discuss this in the following two-part presentation. The first part ("To Become One of Them") was in response to an invitation to give the banquet address at a meeting on international programs of the Western Regional Board of Food and Agricultural Development (BIFAD). I receive many requests to speak at banquets—with the expectation of the sponsors that I will give some comic relief to the attendees. For this speech at the BIFAD meeting, comic relief was out of the question. Our daughter, Karen, had died just six months earlier in Cameroon, West Africa, after two years of volunteer service.

I've harbored strong feelings about foreign service and the necessity for Americans who embark on such a venture to strive diligently to "become one of them." I propose in this presentation selection criteria for such candidates. The speech is not as it was given, in that quotations from Karen's letters are deleted. These quotations appear in the second part ("Grief Is the Price of Loving") in which I discuss my views on facing the overwhelming tragedy of the loss of a child. I hope that it will help others suffering such a fate. Many of Karen's letters have been published in a book by Pacific Lutheran University entitled Dancing in Africa (Bustad, 1985).

To Become One Of Them

Tonight I want to discuss with you who are involved in work associated with the Board of Food and Agricultural Development (BIFAD) an important concept directed toward helping you succeed in your programs designed to help developing countries. *To become one of them* is the subject of my presentation, and the emphasis will be on Africa. I believe, however, that the concept has wider application.

For many years I have been interested in our efforts as a nation to help the less fortunate. This interest, in part, stems from my being a son of immigrant parents and my overseas involvement in World War II in the African, Mediterranean and European theaters of operation. Since that time I have traveled quite extensively and been involved in a great number of international conferences, worked for international organizations, and helped train students from many nations. I also am involved in Amnesty International and Bread for the World which is probably understandable when I tell you I was a prisoner of war in World War II. I've stud-

Presented at Western Regional Board of Food and Agricultural Development Meeting on International Programs, Moscow, Idaho, January 12, 1984.

ied three foreign languages, but I'm proficient in none of them. (The language I'm using tonight is not the first one I learned.) When our children were young we entertained a number of visitors from other countries which probably had some impact on our children, especially one of them whom I will be discussing tonight.

Over many years I've had numerous conversations with a host of people from a number of nations about our country's involvement in overseas programs. We have had many successes as well as failures. I sense our batting average is improving, and I congratulate you for that. How to correct deficiencies must be a major concern of those here tonight. It was a subject that Jim Henson and Jan Noll of the international program office at Washington State University broached with me this spring. The principal thrust of our discussion was how to convey new and necessary information into the hands and heads of those in the Third World who need it and can use it to improve the situation for their communities and their nation, both in the short and long term.

Jan and Jim were interested in our daughter Karen, who was completing her second year as a volunteer teaching a variety of subjects, including English, in a mission school in the Northern Cameroon. (She was due to come back this past summer.) She had special skills in communication, for she was a librarian—a children's librarian, trained at the undergraduate and graduate level in a couple of our nation's best schools. And she had some capability with languages; she handled French reasonably well and overall better than this incident from one of her letters reflects:

> My life this year would make a great movie, except that it would he hard to rate it. It could have all kinds of versions, I guess, depending on what you'd cut out—except the G version or the church group (C?) version would he rather dull, perhaps. Although I don't know, maybe we could play it as comedy. At the moment my latest faux pas is the big joke among the profs. We're having end of the year meetings going down the list of students for each class and deciding whether to promote them. Well, I persisted in mispronouncing baisser (to go down) as baiser (to kiss). I kept saying, "Oh, he baised a lot this term, at least in my class."
>
> They kept straight faces for the first three times but then almost fell out of their chairs they laughed so hard. And they're continuing to laugh. French is still hard for me. I make stupid errors like that all the time.

But then, self-aggrandizement was not one of her faults; self-debasement was. However, her great sense of humor made up for this.

What Jim, Jan and I were planning was to develop a multi-disciplined approach—a team concept involving people skilled not only in the relevant agricultural sciences but in communication, anthropology, the social sciences, philosophy and theology. And the team should have at least one member from the English-speaking world who had become "one of them."

The importance of understanding and empathizing with people of another culture, of becoming one of them, is that it is only then that we can truly help them and learn from them. Unfortunately, many people have lived among members of other cultures and never understood them. Some examples from my limited knowledge of history hopefully will clarify this issue.

Some Jews regard Antiochus IV Epiphanes along with Hitler as the most cruel ruler in the entire recorded history of the Jewish people. Although Alexander the Great had great respect for the Jewish religion and tradition, his reign was followed by a series of rulers whose views differed from his in this regard. From the Jewish viewpoint, the worst of these was Antiochus IV. He added to his name the epithet Epiphanes, which means "the revealed [god]." This name was an anathema to many Jews, and it appeared to many of them that they as a people and a religion would be destroyed, for it seemed this cruel leader was something like Hitler in my lifetime. Antiochus IV set out to eliminate Palestinian Judaism and replace it with Greek religion and culture. He was brutal in his terror against Jews who wouldn't change. If a Jew changed to Greek philosophy and religion, then that Jew was safe.

The Jewish leaders knew they had to do something to give hope to a people oppressed—to keep alive the hope of liberation and of community. And the way they did this was to take stories out of the culture and history of their previous oppressors and overlords—the Babylonians and Persians—and give them a "hidden" theme, a monotheistic theme—a theme that would give hope to them that their God, Yahweh, was God forever and that they would eventually overcome and be free again. But these stories were told in such a way that if one didn't know the Jewish culture and religion, one wouldn't realize it had a hidden message—that it was underground literature. The Book of Daniel in the Old Testament came out of this great persecution. It's referred to as apocalyptic literature—literature that removes the veil a bit, allowing one a momentary glimpse at the future of the cosmos—permitting those sensitive to the hidden meaning to see from the present into a time beyond, a time of liberation to keep their hope alive.

We have a good example of this in our own country during the time of the slave-holding plantation owners. Out of this period grew the Negro spirituals which the white man regarded as innocuous hymns about heaven and the great by-and-by. Although many of these plantation owners had known these slaves all their lives, they didn't realize that when the Blacks sang, "Let us break bread together on our knees," they were giving people instruction on the Underground Railroad; and often when they sang about heaven, they were really singing about Canada and how to get there to the freedom it offered.

This, hopefully, tells us that we must become "one of them" or at least have someone on our team who is "one of them" in order to understand what is really going on.

I admit to great prejudice in this regard, but I believe our daughter was the type of person you should attempt to recruit for a member of this team we're talking about. And I believe Jan and Jim recognized this, as did the people who recruited her originally to come to the Cameroon as a volunteer. So I'll give you a short course on how to become "one of them" as I believe our daughter did. In so doing I will review the qualities and the attitudes and actions of our daughter that made her "one of them." After all, it's hard to argue with success.

1. Karen made a commitment to helping the Third World, most especially Africa. Ever since she was young she had been interested in Africa.

2. She was natively very bright and had formal training in the arts, music, the humanities and sciences. She was schooled in a wide variety of subjects from marine geology to the history of French art.

3. She was trained in library service emphasizing children. If one has the ability to get a message across to children and training and skill in making difficult subjects not only understandable, but interesting and fun, the chances of success in a foreign setting are enhanced.

4. She had a great sense of humor and of community. She had a "wild" imagination, a spirit of adventure and never took herself too seriously.

5. She built bridges instead of barriers in Ngaoundere with all peoples of the community.

6. She appreciated little things, the simple spartan life. She was willing to share what she had and did not care about material possessions. (This meant in the Cameroon: You don't lock your door or flaunt your wealth, e.g., leaving your porch light on all night or driving five times in one day to a town one mile away.)

7. She looked on the assignment as one from which she would learn much more than she could give. She never looked down on these people and she treated them as equals.

8. She spent much more time affirming than infirming her students and co-workers.

9. And she possessed great compassion, reverence and intellectual integrity.

On hearing this you might say, "Where do you find one with these qualifications for our team?" I wish more than anything in this world that our daughter Karen were available for you. Tragically, she is not, for she died suddenly just before she was to come home this past summer. There was no question about her commitment—so vital in such a foreign assignment. In her application form she stated in part:

> I feel that as a Christian I should live simply so that I can more easily identify with the poor and oppressed. Volunteer service is a perfect means to do this, as I will be earning no money to give a false sense of security. I am encouraged in the fellowship of others and I feel a strong call to align myself with the disenfranchised.

She also stated in her application form that she procrastinated and tended to be disorganized. The World Brotherhood Exchange had never seen such frankness in an application form.

Now, you who are here tonight and committed to our country's efforts in improving the lot of the members of the Third World can dismiss my words to you tonight as the babblings of a tired old man in deep grief over the loss of a remarkable daughter. If you do that, I fear for you, for you have failed to realize the importance of becoming "one of them" in your work or having a person on your team who can become "one of them," and you will come to regret this folly in your leisure. And of great consequence to me, you will not only be wasting our nation's resources which are not unlimited, but you will be doing a great disservice to people in desperate need of our help and will have missed a great and rewarding experience for yourself. My fondest wish for each of you involved in foreign service is that your eulogy will be even half as good as our daughter Karen's.

I wish you well.

A postscript. On arriving here this evening I was asked about my commitment to international programs. My response to that is that it would have been much easier for me had I worked very hard for two years in the Cameroon and died there than to have our daughter do that. But then the Cameroonians would have been shortchanged. Grief is the price we pay for loving.

Acknowledgment

The information and advice provided on underground literature by my friends, Dan Erlanger and Will Herzfeld, is gratefully acknowledged. Some of the information on Antiochus IV comes from the *New Testament Era: The World of the Bible from 500 BC to 100 AD* by Bo Reicke (Fortress Press, 1968) and from I & II Maccabees (Deuterocanonical books).

Grief Is The Price Of Loving

Some time ago I heard the following story—I can't remember where or when, but I'm sure I'll never forget it because it addresses all of us who grieve deeply.

In a far-off land a very long time ago, there lived a very wise prince whose life was threatened by revolutionaries. The terrified prince sought sanctuary in a peasant's home under a very big, heavy bed. It wasn't long before the revolutionaries came and beat down the door looking for the prince. They didn't find him, although they went to this bed. Because it was too heavy to move, they shoved swords into it hoping to kill anyone under it. After these revolutionaries left, a very terrified prince came out, and he revealed to the peasant that he was the prince. Because he had been given sanctuary, he would grant the peasant three favors.

The first favor the peasant asked for was that his house, which was very run down, be repaired. The prince said, "You fool, why don't you ask for something more? But your wish will be granted. Now ask for something great." For his second favor he related that he had a little booth down at the market, and the person next to him sold the same produce as he did so he asked for another place further away from his neighbor. The prince said, "You idiot, why do you ask such simple things? But that wish will be granted. Now ask for something real big."

The peasant couldn't contain himself; he asked to know what the prince was thinking about when they were shoving the swords through the bed while he was underneath it. The prince became very angry on hearing this request, and he wanted to know who the peasant thought he was to ask about the emotions of royalty. He then told the peasant that for asking this he would be beheaded in the morning.

So the peasant was taken to prison where he cried most of the night realizing that his life was soon to be over. The next morning the peasant was taken into the courtyard where the executioner was ready. They put the peasant's head on the block and the executioner shouted out, "One! Two!" and before he could say, "Three!" a messenger from the prince came riding up on a horse and said, "Stop, the prince has forgiven the peasant, and here is a note for the peasant." The note said: *Now your third request has been fulfilled.*

Presented in part at the Symposium "Euthanasia in Veterinary Medicine: Anticipatory Grief, the Euthanasia Process, Acute Grief and Bereavement Including Implications for All Medical Disciplines" at Columbia-Presbyterian Medical Center, New York, December, 1984.

You see, the prince knew that there are some things that are so terrible they defy description. And that is how it is with those who have lost someone they loved deeply: *You can't possibly know what it is like until you experience it.*

On July 16, 1983, our daughter died suddenly in Cameroon, West Africa. She was a volunteer teacher who had given up her job to spend two years there, a place where she had found great joy in an accepting community. Since that time I have learned much about grief and grieving. Although I had counseled many people on it before, in many cases I didn't know what I was talking about. Now I am legitimate, but at great cost.

In recalling Karen's death, I identify with Farrell in William Styron's book *Sophie's Choice* (1979). Farrell suddenly cried out in a voice of mingled rage and lament, "'Oh, I *had* a son!...he was a *prince* with language, my son was...some of the letters he wrote—some of those long, knowing, funny, intelligent letters— were the loveliest that ever were written. Oh, he was a *prince* with the language, that boy!...and one of the things that thrilled me was the way he took to books, his gift for words....It was his eye, you see, his eye. He saw things, you understand, saw things that the rest of us don't see and made them fresh and alive.'" And Farrell went on to tell how his son was one of the last marines to die in World War II—not long before he was to come home—and then Farrell closed his soliloquy with these words, "'I don't know why it happened. *God,* I don't know *why* it happened! God, *why?*'" as he wept bitter tears.

Had I been a great writer, I could have written those same words about Karen. She saw things the rest of us didn't see: she was a "princess" with language. When she was young, we insisted she reduce her reading from three books a day. She had a real gift with words. She wrote some remarkable letters to many people—including this one regarding her observations on death:

> I've been thinking about life and death all day today. One of my students died yesterday after a very short, strange illness. He was one of the intelligent troublemakers (as opposed to stupid troublemakers) in this class last year. I was thinking today that I'm sure he's the student I had the most physical contact with last year. I was always pushing him back to his desk and holding him there. And we had verbal battles every day—"Sit down, Mballa....Be quiet, Mballa....Where is your homework?....Oh, and why didn't you do it?..."—ad infinitum...repetitum...ad nauseam.
>
> I've been feeling so sad ever since he died, and my cheeks are beginning to get chapped from the tears. The kids were subdued today, and the teachers who taught him last year, not one had a smile on his face all day; 14 years old is so young to die. I remember a theme he wrote for me last year about the last time he'd been to his village. I remember crying as I read it because they were so happy to see him. And then, after the holiday was over his father cried to see him go, and so did his mother and all of his brothers and sisters. And Mballa cried too, because he loved them and school was so far away from them. The theme was so simple and sensitive—so much at variance with his behavior in the classroom—that I couldn't help but ponder over it a bit. Well, we're all crying again at this newest and longer separation.

> As I was walking home from school today, basking in the sunshine, I couldn't help crying out to God how terrible it was that Mballa would never feel the sunshine on his cheeks again....
>
> There's nothing like a death right in front of you, almost, to make you receptive to really listening. Maybe that's why sometimes life in America gets so trivial and banal—because we aren't close to death the way we are here. So we can ignore questions that concern the meaning of life and death.
>
> I've been thinking of staying another year, but I'm not sure now. Kids are always dying here, and I can't bear to go through it again. Almost every year a student dies at college. Last year it was a student I didn't know so it didn't hit me. Now I know almost all of them and want to think of them all as having bright futures here on earth. I don't want to mourn anymore. I'd rather go home where death is hidden away and the people who die are strangers in the newspaper. I came here to broaden my outlook. First, my kitten died. One morning he's lively and supple and warm in my hands. When I came home from school I picked him up all cold and stiff and hard with ants eating his eyes. That was hard for me. I've had pets die before, but I've never held them in my arms and thrown them down the garbage hole. And now to have Mballa die.

When Karen died, I cannot describe how terrible it was and continues to be. With her death the brightest, clearest, cleverest, most insightful and committed voice in our family had been silenced. I identify with Lord Byron's words: "There is no joy the world can give like that it takes away." When my parents died, they took with them a large part of the past for me. But when Karen died she took a very large portion of the future as well as the past, and that is what makes "the valley of the shadow of death" so incredibly dark and difficult and seemingly unending.

But we can't remain in the valley of the shadow of death forever—we must carry on. For many years of grief counseling I've told people they must carry on. But I didn't know how difficult that was until Karen died. When she died I didn't care whether school kept or not! Everything was ashes, but there were people who were depending on me. We must take care of the living—we must carry on. Separation is a very hazardous thing because when one goes through separation, whether the loss of a child, or a mate by death or divorce, or whatever it might be, one is at great risk from death, from disease, from accidents and one must be aware of that; there is a much higher death rate with such people.

After Karen died I was "going down the tubes" but I had many commitments. I was scheduled at two international meetings. When I arrived at the first one I wasn't sleeping, food didn't taste very good at all, and I was getting weaker and weaker; in fact, so weak I could hardly walk a block. But I finally got a hold of myself, and I said, "You've got to address the issues." You see, I was trying to heal my own grief; one cannot heal one's own grief by nursing it. Only by helping others with their grief can a person heal one's own grief.

Sigmund Freud addressed this issue, too, in a letter he wrote in 1929 to his friend L. Bunswanter who had lost a daughter: "Although we know that after such a loss the acute state of mourning will subside, we also know we shall remain inconsolable and will never find a substitute. No matter what may fill the gap, even if it be filled completely, it nevertheless remains something else." And actually this is how it should be. It is the only way of perpetuating that love which we do not want to relinquish.

Many people have been helped by Rabbi Harold Kushner's best-selling book *When Bad Things Happen to Good People* (1989). Rabbi Kushner recently had an interesting exchange with Dr. Samuel Klagsbrun, a member of the clinical faculty of psychiatry at Columbia University, on "Coping with Suffering," which aired on NBC's Eternal Light program. It helped me because it seemed to me a major segment of our population incorrectly assumed that after the death of a loved one (person or animal), they should eventually get back to "normal." I did not believe that to be the case. In their exchange Rabbi Kushner asked Dr. Klagsbrun if a person ever gets back to normal or really gets over a tragedy like the loss of someone close or a physically disabling illness. Dr. Klagsbrun replied that normality is defined as assimilating—and letting the tragedy affect you for the rest of your life. There will always be a scar! I know in my case, 18 months after our daughter Karen's death, a scar hasn't developed fully yet—there's still a painful raw wound! If I could wipe this tragic loss out of my mind, which I believe would be impossible, I'd be denying it and probably harming myself. In addressing this subject of getting back to normal, Rabbi Kushner said one is not to get back to normal; if one believes they should get back to normal, he thinks they're creating an illusion and so do I.

The majority of people have a difficult time handling grief and consoling grieving people. Those who were most helpful to me were those who had staggered, stumbled and otherwise made their way through the dark valley of death. Instead of offering an assortment of cures or solutions, they chose to share with us our pain and to touch our hurt tenderly with a gentle hand. They join us in acknowledging our own powerlessness when facing death and admitting that they do not understand. They do not busy themselves with trivial tasks, but stand in the face of death together with us as we grieve. These friends remained silent and listened to me as I mumbled on, articulating my own grief. Dr. Paul Tournier, the famous Swiss psychiatrist, impressed upon me many years ago the importance of allowing people to articulate their grief and also to affirm them in moments of despair that accompany great grief.

Now what does all this say about us as we grieve deeply over the death of one of our animals? To me it says that we must be very gentle and understanding to those who grieve following great loss. We must allow them to articulate their grief. An organized support structure is very desirable. In my small hometown we don't have a Betty Carmack, Susan Cohen, Carole Fudin, James Harris, Ralph Holcomb or a Jamie Quackenbush (all expert grief counselors), but we have selected certain sensitive people in our College of Veterinary Medicine and the People-Pet Partnership program who really care about animals and have grieved over the loss of their own animals. We refer people suffering from acute grief to talk to them.

There are two things I instruct people not to say: "It was just an animal" and "What if—" followed by a list of incriminations. Both are destructive and must, therefore, be erased from our vocabulary relative to the death of an animal.

Closure is so important following the death of a love object whether animal or person. When our daughter Karen left for Africa, her good friend and only sister took charge of her dog and her very old cat. Within a year of Karen's death her old cat died, and our daughter Becky was overwhelmed by grief. She cried, "First it's Karen and now her cat!" It was almost more than she could bear. I counseled her about the way to handle the disposition of the body. We discussed what Karen would have done, and we settled on burial at the corner of her little rented beach house where the cat had spent most of her life (certainly the best part of her life), under a tree near bushes and flowers. This was comforting for all of us.

We had a similar and infinitely more difficult problem following the death of our daughter in Africa relative to the disposition of her body. We elected to have Karen buried in Cameroon where she had found such happiness, had so many rewarding experiences and found so many friends and a compassionately concerned community. She had friends among all members of the region, the various nationalities and religions, but most importantly among the children. This fact was obvious at the funeral. The chapel could not accommodate the people who came. To the Africans, the funeral and burial have special significance. In their belief, body-soul become part of them, and the earth and her grave have become sacred ground forever. The grave diggers, desperately poor, refused payment for their work. So we feel that her death, as well as her life, was witness of one committed to promote well-being and self-help of the poor and oppressed—the disenfranchised.

In the published memorial of our daughter written by her colleagues, the final paragraph was of special interest to us. It read in part (translated from French):

> We, African professors, who have enjoyed the friendship and cooperation without crack [without fault] of our colleague and friend have cried with hot tears. As many of you know, this young woman identified herself with us Blacks.

You see, she had become "one of them." This is high tribute.

One of my most memorable luncheons was one we hosted for Dean Rusk, who was Secretary of State for two presidents. When he learned of our daughter's untimely death and the tribute in which her African colleagues said that she became one of them, Rusk responded that he warned his people that they can try to "become one of them," but unfortunately they can't become one of them immunologically.

I close with an excerpt from one of her last letters, which reflects on her reverence:

> Speaking of a dream, I had a strange one the other night. I was at a village market and saw a man holding up some clothes for sale—the long, white robes that men wear here. All of a sudden I felt such a longing, a deep craving for a white robe like that—the sun was hitting the robe so that it shone brilliantly white, almost blinding me with the reflection it was giving off the sun. And I went stumbling up to the man asking how much it was. I was sure that if I could wear a robe like that, so white,

whiter than snow, I would somehow be closer to God. But then I realized that wearing a white robe wouldn't do the trick—that it had to go deeper than that. And in a way, when I turned away from the man and left the robe there, I was disappointed. It would be so much easier to wear a white robe, wouldn't it, than to have a pure heart? I'll never forget that dream. It was so vivid.

Grief is the price of loving.

Although we would give anything to have Karen with us again we realize that this is not to be. We are grateful that we had her on loan for as long as we did (34 years), though she left us before the shadows of life touched noon. This unusually gifted person enriched our lives and the lives of countless others, and we are thankful she utilized her special talents in a place and with a people she felt needed her. It is comforting indeed to know that so many people, most especially children and the young in heart, were singularly blessed by Karen's life.

Writing Your Eulogy

One of my happier experiences is speaking at graduations. Graduations are like birthing—most generally very joyous occasions justifying celebration. I've lost count of how many I've been involved in, but I know of at least 15; I'll recount some of the more unusual ones. I varied the texts and contents, but one of the principal themes relates to the subject of "More Than Scholars" which appears in this volume as a compilation of many presentations with this title. Since 1973 many of the talks were on the subject of "Writing Your Eulogy," and one form of it is included here minus portions that appear in "More Than Scholars."

Most of my graduation addresses have been at colleges and universities, but I have also spoken at several high school graduations. I have spoken to audiences ranging in size from 15,000 at North Carolina State to a handful of "graduates" of a coeducational class in knitting—a hilarious adventure. My own high school finally invited me to give the graduation address some 43 years after I graduated. I told them I had wondered why they hadn't invited me back sooner, but then I realized that before they could do that, they had to wait until several people with good memories died—most especially those who remembered my younger days.

The following is the graduation address which I gave at North Carolina State University, modified slightly to incorporate a few items from other graduation addresses.

Members of the graduating class and all your friends and relatives—that should include everybody here. I am grateful for the kind reception that you have extended to me. It is a privilege to be here with you and to share a few minutes of the rest of your life with you.

This is a great day, probably one of the more memorable days of your life. It is a memorable day for many people because today is the day we turn you loose on the unsuspecting public, and it is to these that I address my remarks. There is relief associated with such an occasion—relief by your parents who have been sending checks rather regularly; by mates who have worked very hard and taken a lot of static from you; and, I'm sure, on the part of some of the professors for what you have given them. And you, I think, are also relieved from having to take any more static from them. So today there are many reasons for celebration.

But I must begin by telling you that the great-out-there isn't a bed of roses. We live in a world that is broken by unshared bread; by the cancer of racism; by pollution that is overwhelming our land, water, and air. There is poverty amid affluence. A surprising number of people have no access to adequate medical care or justice. Corruption is overwhelming our people. We have lost credibility. Compassion is in exile. At a time of burgeoning population, one of our most widespread and serious diseases is loneliness. The frightening specter of nuclear war is ever before us.

Although we have more than our share of problems, we must not despair. For despair is a very great sin. And we do learn from adversity. I believe that it's shape-up time for our country and our society. And during the next few minutes I am going to tell you a few of the things that I think we are going to have to do as we shape up. I have chosen a title for my address that would reflect a synthesis of what I have learned in over 65 years into 15 minutes that may be useful to you. I will address the subject of *writing your eulogy*.

To be a scholar is great, but it is not enough for a good eulogy. Other attributes are necessary, and to make this point I will quote from Charles Darwin's autobiography (1929):

> Up to the age of thirty, or beyond it, poetry of many kinds, such as the works of Milton, Gray, Byron, Wordsworth, Coleridge and Shelley gave me great pleasure.... I have also said that formerly pictures gave me considerable, and music very great delight. But now for many years I cannot endure to read a line of poetry.... My mind seems to have become a kind of machine for grinding general laws out of a large collection of facts, but why this should have caused the atrophy of that part of the brain on which the higher tastes depend, I cannot conceive. A loss of these tastes is a loss of happiness, and may possibly be injurious to the intellect, and more probably to the moral character, by enfeebling the emotional part of our nature.

And he's right. To help to understand this, I'm going to share with you a few of my laws.

I'm not going to give you all 20 of my laws or enlarge upon all of them. I am, however, going to review a few of them by only stating them, and then I will enlarge on the ones that I think are most significant for you for today and for the future.

1. A person's worst difficulties begin when he or she is able to do as he or she likes.
2. Self-discipline is the price of freedom.
3. The true test of freedom is not so much what you are free to do, but what you are free not to do.
4. It is as important to defend human obligations as it is to defend human rights.
5. The trouble ain't that people don't know anything; the trouble is that most of what they know ain't true.
6. To believe that people act logically is illogical.
7. Intelligence can coexist with a want of sensibility and sensitivity.
8. There is no complex problem which, if looked at in the proper way, doesn't become more complex; and the corollary to this is, for every complex problem there is a solution that is simple, neat, and wrong.
9. That mockingbirds sing better if you put out their eyes is not sufficient reason to put out their eyes.

10. You must learn to love or die, and the corollary is, think tough but love tenderly.

The eleventh law that I'll give you without comment is, "If people were born only to be happy, they would not be born to die." That's Alexander Solzhenitsyn's belief, too. I identify with this remarkable Russian in many ways. I, too, at one time learned what it is to be confined in a prison, to learn about freedom the hard way (by losing it), to know what real hunger and cold mean—and those are things that I do not wish on any of you.

During my brief time with you I want to talk to you about your eulogy, from which your epitaph (what is said about you when you die) is extracted. You are now about to begin writing your professional eulogy. It is important that you write it well and that you begin immediately. Several of us have already written most of ours. I've been writing my professional eulogy for 35 years. Some of you won't have 35 years to write yours. I'm very sensitive to this issue for our daughter Karen finished hers suddenly at 34 years of age on July 16, 1983, in Cameroon, West Africa. My hope for each of you is that your eulogy will be as remarkable as hers! This will be difficult because her commitment to the poor and disenfranchised was so very great—it cost her life, her family, and her friends. She was an exceptional human being and great spirit.

There are many great mysteries in life. I wish to begin this discussion by clearing up one mystery for you—what do people wear under their robes at graduation time? At the outset, I must admit that I don't know what all people wear under their robes, but I know what many health professionals wear under theirs, and since you, on this historic occasion, are graduating your first class in veterinary medicine, I thought it appropriate to reveal this mystery to you. Many health professionals wear a T-shirt like the one I'm wearing with the vital instruments and testing equipment in the pockets. And while I'm at it, I should show you what old deans like me wear under their robes: "Old age and treachery will overcome youth and skill." Old Norwegians like me wear a T-shirt with the words "It's hard to be humble when you're Norwegian." But I'm here to tell all of you graduates, not only the veterinarians, that it isn't enough to face tomorrow with appropriate dress, technical skills and instruments, no matter how fancy. It takes something more!

What I want your eulogy to read is that you were whole persons. By whole person I mean a person who possesses compassion, reverence and intellectual integrity, which happens to be one of my most important laws and the only one I will discuss. I will discuss these three components starting with integrity.

Every person has to ask himself or herself whether a thing is right rather than whether it can be done. If I turned any of you graduates loose today, there aren't very many things you couldn't do. But you're to ask yourself first, "Is it right to do so?" You must do that. I can tell you all kinds of stories about people who didn't and regretted such folly in their leisure.

We are plagued by widespread dishonesty today. A recent study of prospective employees in over 700 corporations revealed 42 percent were dishonest, more than two out of five, and the tragedy of this is that without honesty, without integrity, freedom is unsafe; and without freedom it is unsafe to be honest.

At no time in my living memory have I heard the questions raised more often than now: "Who can we believe any more?" and "Who can we trust?" Unfortunately, the answer is, not very many. We have a real crisis in credibility, and it concerns me greatly. Every one of us is responsible for thinking, speaking and acting with integrity so that we really earn and deserve the trust of others. We desperately need credibility because the whole fabric of our society is based on the number of believable people. A society, a community, a profession can exist with only a certain level of skepticism and distrust.

Any profession ceases to deserve respect when its members fail to give honest and first-rate services for a fair price. Only belief and confidence can sustain our common life together, and we desperately need a renewal in these areas if, in fact, we are to have a future. There have to be more names than now given in reply to the question, "Who can you believe any more?" And I would like to place on this list all of you who are graduating here this morning.

The second characteristic of a whole person is reverence. Dr. Albert Schweitzer, one of the truly great men of our age or any age and one of the greatest humanitarians of all time, reminded us of the importance of reverence—about *reverence for life*—which is the name of a course I started many years ago. I believe this is a critical topic for our time—a time in history in this country when weapons of mass destruction are about to overwhelm us. In my generation, more human life was wasted than perhaps at any time in the history of the world. It seems that mass genocide doesn't shake us anymore. And in our own province of responsibility:

- In 1974 we killed 12-15 million dogs and cats in our animal control centers (80% owned by someone—up to 50% with behavior problems).
- A large segment of our population treats animals as disposable, throwaway items. Many animal owners are irresponsible.
- Our elementary school system has little in the way of instruction on proper animal selection and care and our responsibility towards our animals.
- We deny many of our elderly, and many people with disabilities, access to animals. Even well-meaning persons move the elderly into housing units or nursing and retirement homes where no animals are allowed. By taking away their animals, they are taking away from many of them the only thing that is a source of fun and laughter, that gives them unconditional love, that accepts them and makes them feel needed, that socializes them and gives them security, and that provides them with physical contact.

Hear what Albert Schweitzer (1923) says about reverence: "But the ethic of reverence for life constrains all... to give themselves as men to the man who needs human help and sympathy. It does not allow the scholar to live for his science alone, even if he is very useful to the community in doing so.... It demands from all that they should sacrifice a portion of their own lives for others." And he went on to define a person who is ethical. He said "An ethical person is one to whom life, as such, is sacred, animals' lives as well as those of people, and one who devotes himself or herself helpfully to all life that is in need of help." And he said about humane persons, "They feel the happiness in helping living things, and shielding them from suffering and annihilation." We must begin taking killing seriously.

Compassion is the third component of a whole person. I saved it for last because of its overwhelming importance. One of the more remarkable men in my generation in this country was Eric Hoffer, a fellow professor at the University of California in the 1960s—and a longshoreman philosopher. Hoffer (1980) stated, "As things are now, it may well be that the survival of the species will depend on the capacity to foster a boundless capacity for compassion." He was right. It is our last great hope.

Compassion is to suffer with, to have empathy with, and this includes joy and celebration (like today), as well as sorrow. It works from a strength born out of a shared weakness and an awareness of the mutuality of us all. It's the bond between us and also with our animals, and it includes grieving and tasting salt with our fellow men and women. It's a way of life, the basis of community. It's the way to treat all of life: ourselves, our bodies, our dreams, others (both friends and enemies), our animals, our environment, our time and our death. Compassion involves justice-making and caring. I can best describe it by examples.

My first example of compassion came from Bethel in Bielefeld, West Germany. (It appears in the last article in this volume, "Compassion: Our Last Great Hope") My second story is from Loren Eiseley's *Unexpected Universe* (1969) where he captures a great story that I hope you will never forget. I have never forgotten it, even though I may stumble as I tell it to you. It took place on the beach at Costabel one day when he walked along the shore, a shore littered with debris from the sea—debris of life he called it. It seemed to Eiseley that the sea was rejecting its offspring. These life forms would fight their way out to sea only to be cast in again, rejected upon the shore. Among these rejected forms were starfish (or seastars as I've learned they're to be called now). As Eiseley walked along he came upon a stranger who was bent over one of these rejected starfish and he asked him, "Is it alive?" The stranger said yes and then picked it up gently but firmly and cast it far out into the sea with these words: "It will live if the offshore pull is strong enough." And then Eiseley watched this stranger as he walked along the beach throwing back into the sea these rejected, dying starfish. At first Eiseley thought the man was mad, but it wasn't long before he, too, was picking up a rejected starfish and throwing it back into the sea in hopes that it would live again. Eiseley, on recalling this event, said, "Somewhere there is a hurler of stars."

I have told you this to remind you and remind everybody here that the assignment for all of us is to be a more avid hurler of stars, to give others another chance at life. For if you and I are not here to help other people and their animals and keep our environment healthy, there is no just and sufficient reason for us to be here at all. Hail to you, whole persons! Hail to you, star throwers! I wish you well in writing your eulogy—starting now!

Pigs: From BC-2,000 AD— From Outhouse To Penthouse

My fascination with pigs began at an early age and has continued to the present. We always kept a pig or two on the farm. This paper on pigs is abstracted from the original paper (co-authored by Glenn Horstman) which emphasized the nature, cultural aspects and remarkable characteristics of pigs. I've given many talks entitled "My Life With Pigs." It's a more popular talk than "My Life With Norwegians"—and the two should not be confused, nor assumptions made regarding similarities.

I am most grateful to the many people who have helped me understand and appreciate pigs. In addition to the people listed, I thank Drs. Tony Cunha and M.E. Ensminger, and S.A. Palmer, a herdsman in the 1940s at Washington State University. I am grateful to Linda Panepinto and M.E. Tumbleson for their helpful suggestions, and to Plenum Press for giving us permission to publish this abbreviated version. I also thank the many people here in North America and several other countries who have sent me, and continue to send, pig memorabilia and books and articles about pigs.

This presentation will dwell on the pig in our culture, from earliest times through this century, not only to furnish necessary background, but to impress upon everyone here the true nature of this warm, sensitive, clean, intelligent, talented, lovable, loyal, merry, courageous, cosmopolitan creature that has been maligned and maltreated for so long by so many societies. We do this so that, with a new understanding of this remarkable animal, all of you will treat it with the gentleness, reverence and respect that it deserves.

We will begin with a description of where the pig fits into the scheme of things.

Roots Of Pigs

The pig belongs to the order *Artiodactyla*, which includes the camel, cow, giraffe and hippopotamus. The family is *Suidae*. The parent genus and species for the present domestic pig are *Sus scrofa*, the wild pig of Europe, and its close relative, the banded pig of Malaysia, *Sus vittatus*. The latter originated from the Indian Crested Pig, *Sus cristatus*. (Bokonyi, 1974; Clutton-Brock, 1981; Ensminger, 1961; Towne and Wentworth, 1950.)

Abbreviated version of paper published by Plenum Press, NY, in 1986 in *Swine in Biomedical Research* 1:3-15.

The term *hog* may be related to a Hebrew word that means *to encompass* or *surround*, as suggested by the round form of the animal. This is, however, disputed by those who say it is more probably the Arabic sense of the word—to have narrow eyes (Epstein and Bichard, 1984; Mellen, 1952; Youatt and Sidney, 1860).

The word *pig* is derived from the early Middle English *pigge*, which is of dubious origin—probably related to Dutch or Low German. The word *swine* comes from the Old English *swin*, and related forms occur in many languages, such as the Latin *suinus*, the German *schwein*, and the Dutch *zwijn* (Epstein and Bichard, 1984).

Status Of Pigs

The fortunes of the pig have waxed and waned throughout history, but few, if any, fully know the pig (Hedgepeth, 1978; Mellen, 1952; Towne and Wentworth, 1950; Youatt and Sidney, 1860). This lack is well expressed on the back cover of William Hedgepeth's *The Hog Book* (1978): "...here is that forever beguiling creature, the common porker, *Sus domesticus*: the hot-blooded, whole-hearted, intelligent, nimble-footed, fastidious and indefatigable hog that nobody knows." In the limited time allotted, we will attempt to shed much-needed light on the true nature of this beguiling creature.

The hog was held in high esteem among the early nations of Europe, and some ancients paid it divine honors (Barloy, 1978; Ensminger, 1961; Mellen, 1952; Towne and Wentworth, 1950; Youatt and Sidney, 1860). On the island of Crete, pigs were regarded as sacred. Swine were sacrificed by the Greeks for Demeter (the goddess of grain) at the beginning of the harvest and for Bacchus (the god of wine) at the commencement of the vintage. (There was method to their madness, for pigs are equally devastating to growing corn and ripening grapes.)

The Egyptians, the Jews and the Muslims were among the relatively few who abstained from eating pork; in fact, it became an abomination which has more or less persisted to the present time (Mellen, 1952; Towne and Wentworth, 1950; Youatt and Sidney, 1860). For a time, according to Youatt and Sidney (1860) quoting M. Sonnini, the Egyptians were allowed to eat pork on only one day in the year. This day was the feast day of the moon, at which time they sacrificed a number of these animals to that celestial body. If an Egyptian even touched a pig at any other time, he was obliged to plunge into the river Nile, clothes and all, in order to purify himself.

Jewish swine herders were ostracized from society and were forbidden to enter the Temple or to marry into families unassociated with swine (Towne and Wentworth, 1950; Youatt and Sidney, 1860). So great was the detestation in the minds of the Jewish nation regarding this animal that they would not even pollute their lips by pronouncing its name. They would only refer to it as "that beast" or "that thing." In the history of the Maccabees, it is reported that a principal scribe named Eleazer was compelled by the fiercely anti-Semitic Antiochus Epiphanes to open his mouth and accept swine's flesh. He immediately spat it out and proceeded on his own accord to accept torture, choosing to suffer death rather than break divine law and offend his nation (Towne and Wentworth, 1950; Youatt and Sidney, 1860). The Law of Moses (Lev. 11:7, *The Jerusalem Bible*) was very explicit regarding this prohibition: "The pig must be held unclean, because though it has a cloven hoof, divided into two parts, it is not a ruminant." It is of interest to note, however, that Jews, before the time of Isaiah, met secretly in gardens to eat pork and mice as a religious rite. This probably stems from very ancient times when these animals were regarded as divine and were eaten sacramentally as the body and blood of gods (Youatt and Sidney, 1860).

The explanation for the prohibition of eating or touching swine varies. In earliest times it was believed that swine were a source of leprosy; we know now that trichinosis was a problem. Another reason proposed was that swine were filthy and ate food with impurities. Some people would challenge the statement that pigs are not discriminating in their taste. According to Linnaeus, as recorded by Youatt and Sidney (1860), pigs seem to be more discriminating than other domesticated herbivorous animals. This great naturalist stated that:

> The cow eats 276 plants and rejects 218.
> The goat eats 449 plants and rejects 126.
> The sheep eats 387 plants and rejects 141.
> The horse eats 262 plants and rejects 212.
> But the hog eats only 72 plants and rejects 171.

Pigs and people both eat a diversity of items. However, pigs probably come closer to balancing their own ration than most people and other domestic animals. And the pig, given access to a large quantity of feed, will not grossly overeat like most domestic animals and many people.

In spite of the pig's rejection by some people, the fact remains that it has provided sustenance to millions of people in essentially all parts of the world for a long time. The pig is truly adaptable to almost any climate. It is more prolific than any other domestic farm animal except the rabbit, and it quickly attains maturity. This explains its remarkable popularity and its importance in the history of many nations.

The earliest historical records give evidence of the presence of the pig and its use as a prime food source. In many cultures its flesh was highly esteemed. The Romans seem to have made a real art of breeding, rearing and fattening pigs. Every art and skill was applied to develop finer and more delicate flavor to the meat. Sometimes horrible means were applied to gratify the Epicurean tastes and gluttony of certain people. Pliny reported that swine were fed on dried figs and then drenched with honeyed wine in order to produce hypertrophied livers which were apparently considered a delicacy. One of the more famous dishes was named *Porcus Trojanus*, which consisted of a whole hog carcass that was stuffed with thrushes, larks, garden warblers, nightingales and delicacies of every kind. The whole hog was bathed in wine and rich gravies. Another popular dish was a hog served whole with one side boiled and the other roasted (Youatt and Sidney, 1860).

Charles Lamb was exceedingly fond of pigs and of pork, as manifested by the following closing sentences of a letter he wrote on pigs to the famous author Coleridge: "To confess an honest truth, a pig is one of those things I could never think of sending away. Teals, widgeons, snipes, barn door fowl, ducks, geese—your tame villatic things—Welsh mutton, collars of brawn, sturgeons, fresh or pickled, your potted char, Swiss cheese, French pies, early grapes, muscadines, I impart as freely unto my friends as to myself. They are but self extended....But pigs are pigs, and I myself therein am nearest to myself....Yours (short of pig) to command in everything, C.L."

Since pleasant and festive dining stimulates interesting conversation, both in people and pigs, it is appropriate next to discuss language.

Language—Theirs And Ours

The voice and language of the pig, unlike ours and that of other primates, has been little studied. Pigs, however, seem to be in almost constant communication with one another (as well with as the herdperson). They can growl and grunt, squeal and shriek, squeak and snarl, and whine and bark. Little pigs seem to understand an assortment of calls by the mother (Hedgepeth, 1978; Mellen, 1952; Youatt and Sidney, 1860).

There is a general misunderstanding regarding the common call of the pig which has been addressed by Hedgepeth (1978) and noted in 1978 by M. Gartner, then the editor of the *Des Moines Register and Tribune*. Almost everyone believes pigs say *oink*, but they don't. They most often say *gronk*, but when startled they say *rawrk*. They say something like *ronk* when they want an associate to move over and *baawrp* when they're happy. There are also a number of mating sounds, most notably the rutting bark, which is deeper in the boar. And there is a so-called guttural monotone of the baby pig; it squeals when laid on by the mother or otherwise injured. When an intruder appears they say something like *wheeeiii*. When they're grabbed improperly, they squeal "bloody murder." This latter characteristic of pigs tended to discourage scientists from utilizing pigs. The famous Russian physiologist Pavlov had this experience. On hearing of the notable biological benefits of swine as a research animal, he ordered that a pig be introduced into his laboratory. Its shrieking was so disruptive that he banned them from his laboratory with the declaration that all swine were hysterical (Bustad, 1966).

The contribution of "pig talk" to our language is substantial. If one removed from our everyday conversation all references to hogs, pigs or swine, it would be far less colorful, expressive and meaningful. In early American times a "hog" was a 10-cent piece, so that a spendthrift who was willing to spend a whole dime on entertainment was said to "go whole hog." An alternative explanation was that the Romans and other cultures served the animal whole. "Bringing home the bacon" probably derives from the unfortunate greased pig contest when the one who caught the terrorized pig got to take it home. Another explanation for "bringing home the bacon" is of English origin. It grew out of an ancient ceremony which took place annually in the village Dunmow, Essex, 40 miles from London. At this ceremony each couple that had been married one year and that would swear they had been happy and did not wish to be "unmarried" would receive a flitch (or side) of bacon. Ensminger reported that this 700-year-old custom was revived in 1949 (Ensminger, 1961).

"Hog it all" originates from the over-enthusiastic approach that hogs have with regard to their food when it is parceled out in limited quantities. "Eating high on the hog" stems from the fact that desirable roasts and loin chops come from the upper parts of the hog, in contrast to those parts nearer to the ground such as sow belly and pickled pigs' feet which are fare for the proletariat. A "road hog" is one who uses more than the allotted part of the road, while a "pig-headed driver" is excessively obstinate and gives "no quarter." Going "hog wild" applies to many actions, from rapid acceleration when the light turns green to excessive purchases in a bargain basement sale. (Hog Wild is also the name of a business devoted to merchandising pig-labeled material and interesting hog paraphernalia.)

Being "hog-tied" is to be excessively attached to an entity or confined in one's activity due to the over-protectiveness of a mate, mother or manager, or by having all four feet or hands and feet tied together. Many of us are "hog-tied" to our "ham" radio. The term "ham" operator may come from the loquaciousness of amateur radio operators.

Swine are very garrulous and, next to chickens, are the most "talkative" of farm animals. The word "ham" is also used to describe actors and other people who enjoy "hamming it up," which pigs sometimes do also. The origin of this word may be from the early use by actors and actresses of ham fat to remove make-up. If someone is saying something that seems unbelievable, it is referred to as "hogwash." And we express our disdain for something by the phrase "in a pig's eye." The derivation of the phrase "independent as a hog on ice" (Youatt and Sidney, 1860) is obscure. It is generally recognized that a pig strenuously resists stepping on ice.

It is interesting to note that in Webster's unabridged *New 20th Century Dictionary* (2nd edition), of the eleven definitions given for "hog" only one referred specifically to the hog as an animal. Calling a person a hog, pig or swine is considered insulting. To call a person a hog means they take more than their share. Pig has the same connotation, and it is also used to describe policemen as well as girl friends. To say a person's home, room or yard is a pig pen implies that it's dirty and in complete disarray—a real mess! Girls (and, formerly, Chinese males) often wear "pigtails." Boys and girls ride "piggyback;" some people wear "pork-pie hats;" and a lot of people kick and throw the "pigskin" (i.e., the football, which was made from pig skin in earlier times).

As one reads this "pig talk," it's obvious that most of the words and phrases are derogatory. This, I submit, must be changed to reflect the true, beautiful and lovely aspects of pigs. A good place to start is to change the name of the most comfortable shoe available today from "Hush Puppies" to "Hush Piggies," which would denote its principal component, i.e., pig skin. We have gone into many shoe stores asking for hush piggies, and they didn't know what we were talking about until we explained it to the sales personnel. Please join us in this crusade against false advertising.

The last "pig talk" phrase we'll address is one you've probably heard all of your lives: "You can't make a silk purse out of a sow's ear." At the outset we must say this is hogwash. In 1921, Arthur D. Little, Inc., described in some detail in the publication "On Making Silk Purses from Sows' Ears" how they actually made a silk purse out of sows' ears. This purse, modeled after purses used by ladies of great estate in medieval times, is on display in Arthur D. Little's Chemical Museum in Cambridge, Massachusetts. The basic starting material was a glue extracted from

100 pounds of hogs' ears by Wilson and Co. in Chicago. I sent this Arthur D. Little article to Dr. Ed David (one-time presidential science and technology advisor and later president of Exxon Research and Engineering Co.). Ed is an "animal person." The article reminded him of a poem by Ogden Nash:

> The pig, if I am not mistaken,
> Supplies us sausage, ham, and bacon,
> Let others say his heart is big—
> I think it stupid of the pig.

This Ogden Nash contribution serves to introduce the next subject.

Pigs in Literature

There are some very beautiful stories in which pigs are featured subjects. We suspect that everyone here has touched the toes of a child while repeating, to the delight of the child, the famous nursery rhyme: "This little pig went to market, this little pig stayed home." Perhaps less well known are E.B. White's *Charlotte's Web* and *The Death of a Pig*, and R.N. Peck's *A Day No Pigs Would Die*, which we believe should be required reading for everyone.

G.K. Chesterton (1961) understood and appreciated pigs more than most people, and he wrote some beautiful prose about them:

> The actual lines of a pig are among the loveliest and most luxurious in nature. The pig has the same great curves, swift and yet heavy, which we see in rushing water or in a rolling cloud....The beauty of the best pigs lies in the certain sleepy perfection of contour which links them especially to the smooth strength of our south English land in which they live. There are two other things in which one can see this perfect and piggish quality; one is in the silent and smooth swell of the Sussex downs, so enormous and yet so innocent. The other is in the sleek, strong limbs of those beech trees that grow so thick in their valleys. These three holy symbols, the pig, the beech tree, and the chalk down, stand forever as expressing the one thing that England has to say—that power is not inconsistent with kindness.

Pigs do not fare very well, however, in George Orwell's *Animal Farm*. The story is a relatively simple one. The animals take over from Farmer Jones and meet with initial success, but then disaster sets in until the inevitable climax when all the animals regress into worse slavery than they endured under Farmer Jones. The pig, Napoleon, is the chief character; he becomes the dictator, manifesting great wit and cunning. He starts with his ally, Snowball, and his mouthpiece, Squeaker, by masterminding the revolution, then drinking the surplus milk and doing no work. He ends up sleeping in a regular bed, drinking with men and selling animals into human slavery for personal profit. Napoleon shows great lust for power—no animal nature at all. As Margaret Blount (1974) states, "He was a man all the time, leading the trustful animals along the dismal downward path of exploitation, forced confessions, execution, secret police, bureaucracy, extravagance, and bending and reversal of the rules and promises of the glorious revolutionary dawn." The intelligence (or lack thereof) of Napoleon leads into our next subject.

Intelligence Of Pigs

Numerous times we've been asked, "How smart is a pig?" We usually reply that it depends on what questions one asks.

The pig has been regarded as one of the most resourceful, sagacious, and versatile of animals (Book and Bustad, 1974; Britt, 1978; Hedgepeth, 1978; Mellen, 1952; Towne and Wentworth, 1950; Youatt and Sidney, 1860). Mellen (1952) stated that its strategy was appalling. It is a very curious animal; like the cat, it wishes to investigate unfamiliar objects and is very aware of changes made in its environment. And it usually learns in one lesson. Hudson (1919) concluded that it is "the most intelligent of beasts, not excepting the elephant and anthropoid ape—the dog is not to be mentioned in this connection." He observed that pigs of ordinary ability would perform without effort the tricks mastered with difficulty by dogs. Mellen (1952) also described experiments at Yerkes with a multiple-choice apparatus which included 16 compartments. The pigs proved to be the outstanding mammalian performers, surpassing even the higher nonhuman primates in this particular test.

The pig certainly does have versatility. It has been readily trained to hunt and, in fact, may out-perform a dog because of its very keen olfactory system. This special capability has been utilized by truffle hunters in France and Italy. A pig can detect truffles at greater distances than a dog and at an earlier stage of truffle development; therefore it doesn't have to be used as frequently to find available truffles. The pigs involved in this activity, however, have some disadvantages: they become very large and cumbersome to load in the back of a Renault or other small car. And because of their intense fondness for truffles, they are sometimes hard to dissuade from consuming the truffles they find. (Miniature swine might offer some relief in this regard.)

Swine have also been trained as effective "guard" pigs. One such pig was trained to guard a marijuana patch and was reported to have bitten two investigating law officers before being subdued. Pigs have also been used in herding other animals such as cattle. Because pigs have a good sense of time, especially feeding time, they know the appropriate hour when their charges are to be driven home. They are also naturally protective of their own, are very gregarious, and they cooperate with one another starting very early in life. Mellen (1952) reported that older pigs will come to the aid of a troubled comrade.

Pigs might also be useful as search and tracking animals and could probably be trained as "hearing-ear" animals to assist those with hearing disabilities. The development of a small pig would make this more practical. Such a small, well-trained animal might be useful in nursing and convalescent homes for companionship, especially for an agrarian population.

Some pigs seem to have considerable mechanical ability, as evidenced by their facility in opening doors, removing covers from boxes, and opening latches. One pig is reported to have opened nine pens in succession by pushing the latch bolts with its snout. Pigs have been known to shake trees to bring down the ripe fruit. Mellen (1952) reported that pigs have been trained to count, to distinguish letters, colors, symbols, to play dead, draw a cart and walk a tightrope. "Learned pig acts" have appeared at various times for people's entertainment.

For these events, pigs were taught to pick up letters written on cards and arrange them on command. Pigs have also appeared in carnivals and circuses, quite frequently with the circus clown. The only thing that would divert the melancholy of the French King Louis XI was a well-trained troop of gaily dressed pigs who danced to bagpipe music (Youatt and Sidney, 1860).

Hog Calling

Hog calling is an approved rural sport in many regions of our country. It's usually a modification of Swiss yodeling and requires a good deal of skill and, sometimes, ingenuity. It's also very useful and a labor-saving way of rounding up and collecting a herd of pigs. All-American championships have occasionally been held. A panel of judges decide winners, sometimes utilizing a scorecard containing some or all of the following points: (1) strength of tone [20 pts.], (2) quality of tone [20 pts.], (3) originality of call [20 pts.], (4) persuasiveness of call [20 pts.], (5) variety [10 pts.], and (6) command [10 pts.]. Considerable controversy surrounds the appropriate type of call that is most effective. Pigs will respond to an assortment of calls, depending on their training. These could include general voice calls, such as *soooey, whooey, hyyaa,* or *peeg-peeg* (Hedgepeth, 1978; Mellen, 1952; Towne and Wentworth, 1950).

Some pigs respond to their given names like dogs and people. Pigs have also been trained to respond to horns. This method was used in many villages in Germany early in the modern era. Every morning the chief swineherds would walk through the village blowing their horns, and all of the people's pigs would follow the herders to the mountains to forage and then return at night (Youatt and Sidney, 1860). This practice is not utilized very much now because of the cars and trucks whose horns might attract pigs to pursue a speeding vehicle, an activity which could prove to be hazardous for both the pigs and the horn-blowing drivers.

One of the most celebrated stories regarding hog calling relates to a legend of ancient Greece which tells how a pirate ship landed on an island in the Tyrrhenian Sea and stole a large number of pigs. The swineherds were helpless against these pirates, but when the pirates had returned to their ship and were just underway, all the herders called their pigs. All the purloined pigs then crowded to the side of the vessel nearest the shore causing it to list and sink. The pirates and the pigs were all jettisoned; since the pirates couldn't swim, they drowned, while the pigs happily swam to shore and returned to their home shelters in response to well-known calls signifying feeding time (Youatt and Sidney, 1860). This brings to mind the swimming capability of the pig.

Swimming Ability

This species, like many of its wild relatives, is very fond of water. Pigs can obtain food under water, are fond of fish and are capable swimmers. Prehistoric swine probably reached the islands of Madagascar and Melanesia by swimming. Wild hogs have been found on an island off the European continent, a destination they would have had to swim 20-25 miles to reach (Youatt and Sidney, 1860). In Scotland during great floods in the early 1800s, a 6-month-old pig was reported to have swum 4 miles to safety. Pigs also seem to have a keen sense of direction or a homing instinct for they are reported to have found their way home over great distances, by swimming if necessary (Mellen, 1952; Towne and Wentworth, 1950).

In more recent times, during a flood on the Des Moines River in Iowa, a sow and her eight pigs swam safely to high ground when water covered their farm. In 1985 a swimming pig named Priscilla was credited with saving the life of a child with developmental disabilities who ventured too far into Lake Somerville in Houston ("Life-Saving Pig," 1985). The pig, which only weighed 45 pounds, responded to the cries of the boy and was able to tow him (although he weighed almost twice as much as the pig) over 150 feet to shore (and went underwater twice in so doing). The pig's owner reported that the pig had always responded to human cries and would rush to the person to give comfort. Priscilla was the recent recipient of the American Humane Association Stillman Award for heroism. She was the nominee of the Houston Society for the Prevention of Cruelty to Animals. It was the first time a pig had received the award, an honor that received national and international attention.

Cleanliness

Much has been written about cleanliness, or the lack of it, in this species. Under normal conditions, pigs are instinctively neat and fastidiously clean. The pig's reputation for filth and attraction to muddy places stems principally from their need to resort to this for cooling since they do not sweat. However, they much prefer a clean dry bed and are exceedingly fond of comfort and warmth. Ancients observed that when a storm was threatening, pigs would collect straw in their mouths and run about, as if suggesting others do the same, and then make their way to shelter. This apparently is the basis for a Wiltshire saying, "Pigs see the wind." Virgil, too, noted this peculiarity in swine:

> Nor sows unclean are mindful to provide
> Their nestling beds of mouth-collected straw.

Darwin, in his *Zoonomia*, made a similar observation: "It is a sure sign of a cold wind when pigs collect straw in their mouth and run about crying loudly. They would carry it to their beds for warmth..."

Cruelty Toward Pigs

Although pigs have been shown to be intelligent, talented, loyal and sensitive, they have, throughout history, been kicked, whipped, beaten, and otherwise mistreated when kindness, gentleness, and understanding would have resulted in appropriate behavior. Mellen (1952) quoted Sir Francis Head, who observed, "There exists perhaps in creation no animal which has less justice and more injustice shown him than the pig."

Although there were cultures, such as New Guinea tribes, who showed great compassion to pigs, even nursing them on their breasts, our overall record is dismal. The consciousness of people must be aroused and a new ethic of reverence for life must be inculcated in our youth so we don't have modern-day repetitions of the insensitivity manifested in the following incident: During Christopher Columbus' fourth voyage to America, in 1502, when his flagship *Capitana* lay at anchor off the coast of Costa Rica, he received a wild pig as a gift from the natives. On board ship he also had a large spider monkey which had been wounded by a sailor and had one foreleg cut off. Columbus ordered these two animals to be thrown together, and a very bloody fight ensued. All the crew who observed the fight roared with laughter, for compassion and gentleness towards animals was in exile in the 16th century. Columbus thought enough of the incident to mention it in his letter to the Sovereigns as a very novel incident and "such fine sport" (Towne and Wentworth, 1950).

It is time to bring compassion out of exile, not only for the sake of the animals, but for our sake. We need to replace cruelty with gentling.

Significance Of Socialization

The nature of the relationship between a person and his or her animals is of great consequence to the research worker, livestock producer, or any animal owner. We have known for a long time that socialization or gentling an animal (i.e., compassionate handling) has a remarkable effect on the animal's behavior, performance, health and well-being (Bustad, 1983; Bustad and Hines, 1984; Hammet, 1921). This is of special importance in swine because they are very gregarious. They seek out and enjoy body contact and huddle together with other family members. They greatly enjoy being stroked by people once they are gentled and respond remarkably to kind attention.

Few animals known to us are as responsive as the pig to kind treatment nor more deeply resent unkind treatment. A very interesting study performed in Australia reflects the truth of this observation. Hemsworth and associates (Barrett et al., 1984; Hemsworth et al., 1981) exposed 11-week-old gilts to two handling treatments, a pleasant and an unpleasant one, for a period of 11 weeks. The gilts in the pleasant treatment group gained significantly more weight and had a better feed conversion ratio. Members of the unpleasant treatment group had elevated corticosteroid levels and, when bred at their second estrus, their pregnancy rate at two months post-mating was only 33 percent, compared with 87 percent in the gilts in the pleasant treatment groups. These studies, along with many others in different species, show that performance can be remarkably affected by the nature of the treatment accorded an animal (Bustad, 1983; Bustad, 1986; Bustad and Hines, 1984; Hammet, 1921).

Obviously, from the work of Hemsworth and associates, there are significant physiological consequences due to the stress of rejection or separation. We know now, as the result of work in people, that separation and consequent grief results in a significant increase in mortality and in accident rates, as well as increased incidence of disease. There appears to be a syndrome resembling grief in many animals following loss of a close associate, causing the animal to reject food, be depressed and frustrated, angry, and to search almost frantically for the missing animal or person. In some instances, the animal may die. I have addressed this subject, and have given examples of "grief" in animals, including pigs (Bustad, 1983; Bustad, 1986; Bustad and Hines, 1981; Bustad and Hines, 1984).

Pig Records And Pigs As Pets

This paper would not be complete without mentioning some statistics and records set by pigs:

- There are about 800 million pigs in the world today (Epstein and Bichard, 1984).
- The oldest pig on record was 27 years (Altman and Dittmer, 1972).
- The largest pig on record weighed 1,904 pounds (Hedgepeth, 1978).
- The largest litter was 34 piglets (Hedgepeth, 1978).
- The most matings by a boar in a 24-hour period was 25 (Hedgepeth, 1978).
- Pig squeals range from 100-115 decibels (compared to 112 for supersonic Concorde jet at takeoff) (Britt, 1978).
- Prominent people who have had pigs as pets include Sir Walter Scott, President Abraham Lincoln and U. S. Senator Mark Hatfield. The famous writer G.K. Chesterton may have had a pet pig, for he stated, "I could never imagine why pigs should not be kept as pets."

Conclusion

I spent my childhood and youth in a Scandinavian community and have often recalled how impressed I was at how the pigs I helped raise on the farm resembled the Norwegians who resided in the community. By this I mean that both species are:

> Temperate at the trough,
>
> neat and clean if given the chance, and
>
> dignified in courtship and marriage.

On the basis of this presentation I hope you now realize these statements are very applicable to pigs.

During the long and often disturbing history of the pig, it has obviously spent more time in the "outhouse" than in the "penthouse." I hope that as a result of the information I have presented, you will not only appreciate that the pig belongs in the penthouse, but that you will help to provide the care and attention dictated by one who inhabits this elevated station in life.

Our Responsibilities
To The Natural World

For more than three decades I have been concerned about our deteriorating environment and have addressed this subject in many forums—principally at Holden Village, an international dialogue center in the Wenatchee National Forest near Chelan, Washington. My article here is an "unabridged" version of an editorial that appeared in Anthrozoös, the journal of Delta Society. We are approaching a crisis relative to our natural environment which must be addressed globally!

*D*elta Society is committed to the exploration of the interaction of people, animals and the environment. Our major emphasis has been on people-animal interactions. In order to address the third component, our conference topic for our 1988 annual meeting was People-Animals-Environment: Exploring Our Interdependence. The unanimous choice as keynote speaker was Dr. Michael Robinson, director of the Smithsonian National Zoological Park. He was a popular choice because of his plenary address on "Zoos: Today and Tomorrow" at our 1987 annual meeting in Vancouver, British Columbia (Robinson, 1988). An important consideration, too, was his long experience working in the tropical rainforest, his many publications on this important subject, and his recent article in *BioScience* on "Bioscience Education Through Bioparks" (Robinson, 1988a). His topic was "What Are Our Responsibilities to the Natural World: Should We Save the Rainforests?" Because his presentation was so well received and because there were so many requests for a copy of his paper, I asked that he submit his manuscript for publication in *Anthrozoös* (Robinson, 1989).

Our *Anthrozoös* editor, Dr. Andrew Rowan, asked me to respond to Dr. Michael Robinson's manuscript; I am pleased to do that. Regarding Michael Robinson's question, "Should we save the rainforests?" the answer of the conference attendees would be a resounding yes. He addressed in a commendable manner the Delta triangle (people-animals-environment) and admirably demonstrated the complexity of this interaction. Although a 45-minute talk is a very limited time allotment for addressing tropical rainforest conservation, Dr. Robinson managed to do just that and also provided us with an impressive list of useful references.

Paper first published in 1989 in Delta Society's journal, *Anthrozoös* 2(4): 219-220. Reprinted with permission.

Dr. Robinson reminded those who heard him of some sobering information:

- No other animal has permanently altered the properties of species of other life forms (as we have).
- Early humans struggled against nature; now nature is struggling for survival against humans.
- Our rainforests are the last unspoiled terrestrial ecosystem and are in grave danger of falling before our technology, which is applied to the process of sustaining our population growth at ever-increasing levels of resource consumption.
- We are not only draining our fossilized resources and other non-renewable resources, but we are agents of meteorological change including global warming.
- No living force has destroyed species in such a brief time-span with such irrevocable effect as we are now doing.
- Unlike cataclysmic geological forces (like death stars) implicated in extinctions of early times, our destruction is limited not to millions of years but to 100-200 years.

Michael Robinson's summary of the nature of the destruction and loss estimates by a number of people and organizations lends credence to his concerns—including:

- 25-40 percent of the original extent of the tropical forest was gone by 1980 and 1 to 1 1/2 times the amount already lost (80,000 square kilometers) was estimated by the World Resources Institute as damaged.
- Tropical rainforests are the habitat of 90 percent of all terrestrial animal species.
- Norman Meyers estimated from analysis of disaster hot spots in tropical forests that 10 areas studied are likely to lose 90 percent of their forests by the year 2000. Such destruction would cause the loss of 7 percent of the earth's plant species and at least a similar proportion of animals. The area of concern represents only 0.2 percent of the earth's land surface.
- Recently I was told that we are losing tropical rainforests at the rate of 60 or more acres per minute.
- The World Resources Institute reported that air pollution is killing forests and causing $5 billion in crop losses each year.

I am impressed with the seriousness of the destruction. More and more people are asking why. When I finished reading Dr. Robinson's manuscript, I went to my file and found a talk I gave in 1974 at our college's 75th anniversary on "Bombs, Bulldozers, Babies, Bread and Baloney—Our Five Biggest Problems." In that talk I expressed my grave concerns about our depleting natural resources, our energy sources, our diminishing environmental quality, our burgeoning population outgrowing the food supply and our ignorance and misinformation about the issues.

I am dismayed that so little has been done in the 15 intervening years. The time, it seems, was one of sleep. In my introduction, I recalled a particular comic strip by Walt Kelly, creator of *Pogo*. The scene was set at the Okefenokee Swamp; Pogo and his friends are having a party. "Here's to each and all, bless them. Here,

here, come on Albert. Toast up." Albert says, "I am still brooding about pollution. All them characters what's dump anything anywhere. They is enemies of the people." He flings his cigar butt, which ends up in their lemonade supply. Pogo hollers, "Albert!" Porky says, "We have met the enemy, and he is us."

More and more people are coming to realize that we are the culprits, and only we can prevent the impending disaster. In the 15 years that have passed between my proletarian address and Dr. Robinson's erudite presentation, the situation has not improved—in fact, it has worsened. Population and pollution are still increasing, and destruction of species continues unabated.

Michael Robinson noted that a fundamental problem is procreation—a population increase that is out of control. So many people either fail to comprehend the concept of exponential growth or don't believe it's really happening. To make the point I often tell illustrative stories. One of them is about the person who had a lovely pond on his farm. He was very fond of water lilies, so he obtained a water lily that doubled in growth every day. In 30 days, the pond was completely covered by water lilies. The obvious questions is: "When was it only half full of water lilies?" The answer is of course: "The day before it was fully covered with water lilies." It happened fast. That's exponential growth. And that's what the population is doing in many places. The real tragedy is that even now our food production is not keeping up with population growth.

Michael Robinson stressed that people must recognize that local and regional problems (e.g., destruction of rainforests) are part of a larger problem—a global issue. The interrelationships are very complex. Michael Robinson didn't stop with reciting a litany of the destructive processes that threaten our very future. He devoted a good deal of time and pages suggesting alternatives to destruction.

He makes a plea for a Manhattan Project-type approach to tropical biology, i.e., an all-out effort in world community. It is urgent that we obtain a moratorium on rainforest destruction. This action will meet strong opposition in some quarters, as evidenced by the recent murder of an activist for forest preservation in Brazil. We will need wise and practical people to address all aspects of the issues.

Recently, Jonathan Roughgarden (1989) proposed that Congress create a U.S. Ecological Survey (USES). And he makes a strong case for it. I sense Michael Robinson's Manhattan Project-type approach would opt for global extension, and I agree. I propose on that basis that a World Ecological Survey (WES) be formed under the United Nations or other auspices that would have the resources to purchase lands the way the Nature Conservancy does for preserving them.

I believe some good things are happening, and that there is a growing awareness of the serious problems we face. When Michael Robinson's manuscript arrived, my desk was piled high with letters, announcements, requests for funds and many magazines and journals that had accumulated during my many absences. A significant number of these communications addressed the subjects referred to by Dr. Robinson. There was *Climate Alert* which summarized the Toronto Climate Conference that called for 20 percent cutbacks in global carbon dioxide emissions. They also called for the creation of a World Atmosphere Fund to address how to reduce greenhouse gas emissions. This publication included the program for the December 1988 Second North American Conference on

Preparing for Climate Change! It also listed 15 scheduled meetings for 1989 in various countries of the world discussing climate-related subjects.

And there was the winter edition of *Tropicus,* a publication of Conservation International (C.I.). It included an interesting interview with a C.I. vice president, Jack Hood Vaughn, who has spent most of his life in Latin America, first in foreign assistance work, and later as director of the Peace Corps and ambassador to both Panama and Colombia (Vaughn, 1989). He said 20 years ago people in Bolivia and Mexico thought the jungle would go on forever, their rivers would stay clean and the topsoil would stay in place. Now they know that isn't true as they witness pollution of air and water and extensive erosion.

Mr. Vaughn went on to state how technology has complicated their problems. The World Bank financed the Rondonia highway. He said it cost a half billion dollars to build this highway to nowhere; it enticed hundreds of thousands of squatters who were attracted to the new frontier. They came, slashed and burned, and experienced a new despair—there was no topsoil, and they were worse off than when they came (and so was the environment).

Many more journals and reports posed questions on environmental issues such as: "Is our climate out of control?" and "Is the greenhouse effect for real?" *The New York Times* usually devotes two columns to environmental issues daily. On the day I completed this editorial I received a letter from the New Forest Fund containing seeds of the Leucaena tree. I was directed to plant them to help stop the deadly greenhouse effect.

It's well we have this exposure and education process. Michael Robinson reminds us of the "enlightenment fallacy" trap: that education will solve the problem. Ignorance is not the only or basic cause. In Michael Robinson's view the basic causes are greed, need and poverty, and that's what we must attack. But that isn't to say we shouldn't continue our educational programs.

Many believe economic development can and must provide for sustainable life, and, furthermore, that conservation of nature can't happen unless the needs of people, i.e., poverty and suffering, are addressed. It seems almost everyone agrees that population pressures are a critical issue and in many places spell doom for people, animals and the environment. But these population pressures will continue until we do something about poverty and suffering. On the basis of experience in most societies, when basic needs are provided and economic development occurs, birth rates fall. But this economic development must go hand-in-hand with wise conservation measures.

The monetary debt and high interest rates that weigh so heavily on the Third World nations where the tropical rainforests are in jeopardy is a problem that must be addressed far more vigorously. If not addressed, hunger, poverty, suffering and high birth rates will continue and the future of planet Earth is in jeopardy. When we go to these areas to modify prevailing practices, we must involve the indigenous people and take into consideration their way of life. Conservation and economic goals must involve the local inhabitants, an issue Michael Robinson supports. I am pleased that new initiatives are being discussed relative to debtor nations. For example, banks holding loans could provide incentives for debtor nations to change their present practices and implement the issues I have just discussed.

I referred to Pogo's classic statement earlier regarding discovery of us as the enemy. We must all become conservationists, tree planters and energy conservers, most especially of hydrocarbon fuels. We are consuming these fuels now as if there's an unlimited supply—leaving our children and our children's children dispossessed. Supplies of fuels are finite.

The seriousness of the problem is of such dimension as to call for a change in national and international priorities. The United States and other countries are considering manned space flights to Mars at a tremendous cost. This is proposed at a time when we have defined only about 1.6 million species of organisms on our planet. The recent estimates of the number of species is upwards of 20 or even 30 million. We speak about loss of species, but have only a small percentage of them defined. Certainly addressing this great deficiency in our knowledge is far more critical to the future of the planet and its inhabitants than sending people to Mars. Billions could be saved to fund world ecological surveys and for economic development in Third World countries.

My friend Aaron Katcher, a psychiatrist at the University of Pennsylvania, sent me a letter saying he had been reading a sad but fascinating book by Catherine Caulfield (1984) called *In the Rainforest*. He went on to quote the following account which addresses the issue poignantly:

> The villagers, who had recently suffered several years of terrible flooding that they attributed to government-licensed deforestation, decided to protest. In March, Prasad-Bhatt declared: "Let them know they will not fell a single tree without felling one of us first. When the men raise their axes, we will embrace the trees to protect them." The trees were spared and the Chipko Andolan (the Hugging Movement) was born.

Aaron then went on to say that people have to be attracted towards the conservation of the natural world with the direct kind of physical and emotional engagement that the idea of hugging a tree implies.

In closing I recall what J. Sommer stated on a television program, "We are all endowed with a wonderful gift, the human brain. Within it lies the promise and triumph of our species. Out of these billions of cells (in our three-pound brain) emerged the insights that have changed the course of human history." On it depends our hopes for better tomorrows for people, animals and our natural environment (and that includes our tropical rainforests).

And now I close for I must go and tend my potted Leucaena trees!

Recent Discoveries About Our Relationships With The Natural World

The most memorable event for those involved in exploring the interactions of people, animals and the environment was the Fifth International Conference on the Relationship Between Humans and Animals in November 1989 in Monaco. It was exceedingly well planned, organized and implemented by Tristan Follin and Professor Hubert Montagner. The Honorary Chair for the conference, the charming Princess Antoinette, is a true believer in the "movement." She's a great force in the principality for the well-being of people and animals.

There were over 600 attendees from 24 countries and more than 190 speakers. A year before the meeting I was asked to summarize the first two days of the conference. I told the planners Bruce Fogle was a master at such an assignment, and I was right. So I was given the assignment of giving the final Plenary Address on noteworthy developments during the previous decade and a charge for the next one.

Clinical observations and the results of recent research lend credibility to the centuries-old belief that the association of people with animals and the natural environment contributes to overall health and well-being. Recently we have "rediscovered" that a close relationship between people and the natural environment, most especially animals, is vital to the well-being of our planet, its inhabitants and its habitat. This relationship helps fulfill our inherent need to nurture. The roots of this relationship, often referred to as a "bond," go back thousands of years; but urbanization, industrialization, mechanization and other forces have caused the diminution of the opportunities for nurturing and affectionate interaction with people and our natural surroundings. This deprivation of nurturing opportunities has resulted in increased stress and consequent challenges to our health.

This unhealthy state of affairs is being vigorously addressed by many people in many disciplines with the object of helping to restore health to communities everywhere. We in the Delta Society and in our sister organizations in other countries are directing our efforts to these ends by exploring the interaction of people, animals and the environment through scientific study, service and teaching.

Condensed and updated version of the presentation given at the Fifth International Conference on The Relationship Between Humans and Animals in Monaco, November 15-18, 1989.

In the past two decades research and clinical observations have shown that animal association may contribute to:

• Higher one-year survival rates following coronary heart disease (Friedmann et al., 1980; Friedmann and Thomas, 1995)

• Reduction in blood pressure and stress level in healthy subjects, as well as changes in speech pattern and facial expression , and lower plasma triglyceride and cholesterol levels (Baun et al., 1984; Katcher et al., 1984; Katcher, 1987; Wilson, 1991; Allen et al., 1991; Anderson et al., 1992)

• Improvement in quality of life for elderly persons (Robb, 1987; Stallones, 1990)

• Socialization of young children with their peers (Hart et al., 1987; Nielsen and Delude, 1989)

• Development of nurturing behavior and humane attitudes in children who may grow to be more nurturing adults (Melson, 1990; Ascione, 1992)

• A sense of constancy for foster children (Hutton, 1985)

• More appropriate social behavior in mentally impaired elderly people and prisoners (Burke et al., 1988; Jecs, Dawn, personal communication; Lee, David, personal communication; Hendy, 1984; Katcher et al., 1989)

• Success in psychotherapy sessions and in psychiatric institutions in helping patients work through their anxiety and despair (Peacock, 1984; Beck et al., 1986; Holcomb and Meacham, 1989)

• Improved balance, coordination, mobility, muscular strength, posture and language ability as a result of therapeutic horseback riding (ITRC, 1988; Biery and Kauffman, 1989; Dismuke, 1984)

• Reduction in the demand for physicians' services for medically nonserious problems among Medicare enrollees, and an apparent buffering effect against psychological stress (Siegel, 1990; Siegel, 1993)

• Facilitation of social interaction between strangers (Hunt et al., 1992)

• Highly significant reduction in minor health problems and highly significant improvement in psychological components of general health, plus a dramatic increase in recreational walks by dog-owners (Serpell, 1991)

• Encouragement of preadolescents' emotional reciprocity and caring responsibility, as well as lessening feelings of loneliness (Davis and McCreary Juhasz, 1995)

Those studying the interactions between people, animals and the natural environment find it very difficult to overestimate the significance of animals in the lives of people everywhere (Anderson, 1975; Anderson et al., 1984; Arkow, 1986, 1989; Fogle, 1981, 1983, 1986; IIRHPR, 1985; Katcher and Beck, 1983; Rowan, 1988; and Delta Annual Meeting Abstracts and the journal *Anthrozoös*). The number of animals in our society is impressive. At this time, the generally cited number of dogs in the U.S. is 55 million, and of cats 60 million. Determining the number of cats is especially difficult because many people feed free-ranging cats that are not officially claimed by anyone. In this regard, the number of stray and feral cats is estimated at 25-40 million. This number is not included in the owned population. Researchers are now addressing the problems inherent in estimating dog and cat populations and have proposed ways to arrive at more realistic population data (Patronek and Glickman, 1994; Patronek, 1995; Patronek and Rowan, 1995).

Even homeless men and women often contrive to maintain pets whose affection and companionship are highly important to them (Kidd and Kidd, 1994). This has been recognized in England, where the Hope Project was started in 1991 to provide veterinary services to homeless people with dogs, including vaccination, worming, flea prevention and free neutering (Kase, 1996). Beginning in London, this project has been extended to other cities.

Animals (or their images) often appear in art, comics, celebrations, dreams (up to 57 percent of dreams of 4-year-old boys involve animals, according to Van de Castle, 1983), fables, folklore, food, imagination, language, medicine, music, photographs, religion, wishes, work and worries. At long last, animals are gaining some legitimate recognition among more and more members of the professions involved in providing health care. In fact, we are reaching a point where, for some conditions, animal interaction is the therapy of choice.

The importance of animals to the well-being of people is becoming more and more evident. This is especially true as we realize that at no time in history have so many members of Western society been devoid of healthy interaction among themselves and with the environment. More and more people are electing to live alone; many who are married choose not to have children. Singles or couples who have children are compartmentalized. Many fathers and mothers work outside the home, usually in different locations and sometimes on different schedules. Children are usually born in a hospital, spend a great deal of time in daycare centers, and then proceed to kindergarten, elementary school and high school—usually all in different locations (the one-room school I attended is a thing of the past). When at home, children are watching television or wearing headphones attached to a source of sound, usually loud music. This deprivation of nurturing opportunities and compartmentalization has resulted in increased stress, depression, loneliness, and overall serious challenges to the health and well-being of a significant segment of our population. Companion animals have refused compartmentalization and serve as nurturers for many people; they also are objects of nurture, promoting touching, playing, and sharing with few time restraints.

In a study of a multi-ethnic sample of 877 Los Angeles County adolescents (Siegel, 1995) about half lived in households that owned pets. Among the pet owners, 64% reported that their pets were very or extremely important to them; only 10% said the pets were "not at all" or "not too" important. Adolescents with no siblings living at home rated their pets as more important than did others; so did those with sole responsibility for care of the pet.

Many studies demonstrate the importance of touch in human-animal interactions. Aaron Katcher has been an articulate spokesman relative to the importance of touch; he reminded us (Katcher, 1981) that in the English language, a companion animal is a "pet" which means to touch and caress. He found that although men in Western societies initiate and respond to touching much less frequently than women, in waiting rooms of veterinary clinics there were no differences between men and women in the frequency, amount and kind of touching of their pets. It seems that dogs, and possibly other animals, serve as appropriate and safe objects of nurture through which both men and women can express and receive affection, even in public.

Children, especially males, when they reach the ages from 5 to 8, decline and even resist physical contact by and between parents or other adults. But Katcher suggests that the presence of a pet can renew the joys of touch for the child who can set the "rules" and time and nature of affectionate displays.

I believe there is overwhelming evidence that human health and well-being depend on the quality of social interrelationships (significantly touch) through-out life (House et al., 1988; Lynch, 1977). One of the most impressive examples of this is the dire effect on infants resulting from lack of contact with mothers, a condition seen in both humans and animals (Pauk et al, 1986; Schanberg and Field, 1987; Bartolme et al, 1987, 1989; Barnes, 1988; Katcher, 1988). When social contact is absent, infants have been seen to manifest an immobilization response with decreased activity and sensitivity, increased secretion of endor-phins and concomitant decrease in the secretion of growth hormone.

In many domestic animals, as well as other mammals (Bustad, 1987) and birds (Gross and Siegel, 1982), gentle handling and social contact increase their resistance to diseases, their survival from major surgery, their growth, efficiency of feed utiliza-tion and conception rate, and makes them more relaxed and more easily handled. Of significance, too, is the psychophysiological response to contact comfort that per-sists into adulthood. A study of beef and dairy cows (Sato et al., 1993) showed that closely related and same-age cows licked each other most often, but such grooming was also frequent among others in the herd. The researchers suggest that grooming contact may reinforce social bonds and suppress aggressiveness.

As Katcher (1988) has noted "...the process of giving care to others, the acts of nurturing, touching, holding, protecting, giving food, and guiding, evoked the same feelings, and the same physiological events as being nurtured. In its most simple form, when we care for others we feel as if we are cared for. That is why owners are so certain that their pets give them overwhelming love." In my obser-vations, nurturing a significant other can relieve depression and loneliness.

Recommendations

Our knowledge and understanding of the critical importance of the human-ani-mal bond to individuals and to society is steadily increasing. As we become more aware of the importance of this interaction, we must begin to formulate ideas and programs, such as those outlined below, which will serve to promote the human-animal-environment bond. The following are but a few of the programs of service and teaching that we can implement in this regard.

• Increase support of a data-based research effort on human-animal interac-tions and animal-assisted therapy (Beck and Rowan, 1994). For example, there are studies that suggest a link between closely bonded companion ani-mals and the long-term health and well-being of people. Because of the cost and complexity involved in a long-term definitive study, it is recommended that existing large epidemiological studies be re-examined and follow-up data be obtained pertaining to any linkage of disease incidence (e.g., cardiovascu-lar disease) and the presence or absence of a closely bonded animal. Future national health surveys should include questions related to the presence or absence of closely bonded animals. Longitudinal studies are a must.

- Expand prison programs involving animals. For example, in a program involving selected maximum security prisoners that train animals to assist people who have disabilities, dogs have been trained to alert their seizure-prone owners to an imminent seizure. This remarkable finding needs to be investigated to determine how to pre-select such dogs for training and what type of training methods should be utilized.
- In conjoint efforts with authorities and qualified personnel, establish criteria for certification of all classifications of service animals. This certification should also include animal-assisted therapists and animal trainers.
- Promote programs that train certified service animals. An important new study (Allen and Blascovich, 1996) found substantial economic as well as psychological and social benefits when wheelchair mobile individuals with major disabilities were provided with service dogs. Costs per week for paid assistance decreased by 68%. Allowing for the cost of training and maintaining the dogs, this could result in an estimated net savings of $55,000 to $92,000 per person in eight years (estimated service period of a dog). Other researchers have found evidence that people without disabilities react less negatively toward those with disabilities when the latter are accompanied by service dogs (Mader and Hart, 1989; Eddy et al., 1988; Valentine et al., 1993).
- Develop strategies for third-party payments for animal-assisted therapy.
- Educate authorities regarding the need many people have for close attachment to an animal. Through information sessions, publication, and consultancy to legislative bodies, make it possible for more people to have legal access to close animal interaction and train animal owners in responsible animal care and obedience training of their dogs (see Hart et al., 1985).
- Encourage the development of bioparks as described and promoted by Dr. Michael Robinson (1988a), director of the Smithsonian Institution's Washington Zoo. These bioparks would serve to educate children and adults, giving them real hands-on experience in converted zoological gardens where visitors would learn about animals not only by sight and sound but also by smell and touch. Such exposure, properly organized and implemented, could fulfill some of our recommendations.
- It is a matter of urgency that the education and training effort be improved and expanded in several areas, including:
  1. Education of youth in practical aspects of nurturing one another, animals and our natural environment.
  2. Training of veterinarians, animal technicians, social workers, and health care professionals in grief counseling for those who have suffered the loss of closely bonded animals. We should also encourage more groups to form regular grief-counseling sessions.
- There is an increasing need to address the plight of AIDS (acquired immunodeficiency syndrome) victims, most especially children. Many AIDS patients could benefit by animal association. Authorities should be informed that removing companion animals from these patients would accomplish very lit-

tle in eliminating disease, and would remove for some the only source of unconditional love, security, acceptance, forgiveness, fun and touch. Well-screened healthy animals should be made available, along with informed, well-trained volunteers committed to helping in this effort. Delta Society has information available on the subject of animals and AIDS.

The consequences of loss of suitable objects of nurture have been inestimable, and to counteract this downward spiral, we must also mobilize our communities to address this situation now and for the future. I naively propose a solution that is unique in today's world in that it will be fun and the cost will be modest.

The solution proposed is to bring nurturing instruction into the elementary and secondary school system. Children should be taught to care for living things including each other, animals, plants, soil and the environment—to become stewards of this planet by "hands-on" experience in tending the earth and its creatures. Involving students in a "big brother" and "big sister" arrangement for care and instruction at all grade levels in nurturing of animals and plants will promote cooperation, compassion and enhance nurturing skills. Group projects in each class should also be promoted, as well as projects which involve animals in their natural habitat. As Konrad Lorenz, to whom we pay tribute at this conference, taught us, we could learn a great deal more about animals by observing them in their natural habitat.

As a result of 10 years experience with our curriculum, *Learning and Living Together—Building the Human Animal Bond* (Vaughan et al., 1986), we have found it to be helpful in teaching children from preschool to the 6th grade. Additional lessons on Reverence for Life, Behavior of Animals and Tending the Earth are being considered for later inclusion. I also initiated a course entitled "Reverence for Life" which I have taught at the university level for more than fifteen years. (A brief outline of the course is included in the Appendix.)

Other beneficial programs have been instituted at Canyon Park Elementary School in Santee, California, at Gullett Elementary School in Austin, Texas, and at the Ott Elementary School in Phoenix, Arizona (Kaye, 1984). Additional programs have been discussed in the Delta Society magazine *People, Animals, Environment* (1987 and 1988 Spring editions), including reports on interesting programs in the U.S., South Africa and Belgium.

Another outstanding model for children and youth is the one developed by Dr. Sam Ross and his associates at Green Chimneys in Brewster, New York, to address the needs of vulnerable children and teenagers from the inner city. These youngsters have learned the rewards of nurturing, including gaining competence in farm-related tasks, thereby enhancing self-esteem and developing a reverence for all of life. This is a far better choice than dropping out of school for careers in crime, addiction and violence, options which compromise health and lead to an early death. The Green Chimneys experience should have wide appeal and broad application. It could well serve as a national, even a world, model for the general reform of education starting with the very young (Ross 1981; Ross et al, 1984).

Admittedly, there's a big jump from a child learning nurture of a guinea pig in a classroom to saving the rainforest. However, nurturing one another and animals and plants and practicing conservation is a big first step. Paraphrasing Dr.

Katcher, proper care of the family pet is the first lesson in the book of environmental ethics (Katcher, 1988). We must immerse students in living things. The growing interest in nourishing and caring for plants and animals must be encouraged, especially in our children, for we need to preserve and care for the life of the entire planet.

Recently, we have come to realize how fragile our planet is (Robinson, 1989). Children must come to realize that nature is not an enemy to conquer, but an entity in need of tender care and concern. Our future together here on planet Earth depends upon our addressing this need with careful haste. Animal, plant and soil specialists at the local level need to work together with educators, health professionals, lawyers, philosophers, politicians, scientists (including molecular biologists) and theologians to implement such a program (see Wilson, 1989 and other articles in the September, 1989 issue of *Scientific American*).

National and world priorities must be reordered to address a great deficiency on planet Earth (Bustad, 1989). At a time when nations are planning cooperative efforts to place people on Mars, the very future of the health and well-being on our own planet is in jeopardy. We have defined and described probably less than 10% of the species on planet Earth. There are frequent reports that list the number of species on the endangered list or that are now extinct. The truth is that we really don't know how many species are endangered or lost because we don't know what we have.

We are now at a time where we are experiencing not only an increased cooperation between nations, but also a growing sensitivity and reverence for life and a greater interest in curricular change in our school systems. We must take this opportunity to promote international cooperation in defining our species, and to work together in nurturing people, animals, plants and our environment, thereby contributing to a secure future for this planet. With an emphasis on nurture of people, animals and environment, chances of attaining peace will also be greatly enhanced. Animals and children can help promote a state of peaceful coexistence between people and the rest of this remarkable planet.

I believe, as I conclude, that an interesting area with great potential for benefiting and enriching the lives and conditions of people and animals is opening to us in research, service and teaching. By working with colleagues worldwide in a variety of disciplines, we can develop new and creative ways to realize the great potential inherent in people-animal-environmental interactions properly studied and utilized. On the basis of my experience for the last two decades, I am devoting my remaining days to this adventure—a call for compassion, educated concern, nurturance and its early incorporation into our educational curriculum, and reverence for all of life. My plea is that we heed the words of Alfred Tennyson: "Come, my friends, 'tis not too late to seek a newer world."

Compassion: Our Last Great Hope

My parents manifested compassion as did my grandmother, something for which I'm eternally grateful. Unfortunately I haven't always been kind and compassionate, but I've respected those who are. My mother kept reminding me of the biblical admonition, "Be compassionate as your heavenly Father is compassionate." It was a tall order. Many years ago I began collecting information on compassion for people and animals.

In response to a request to speak at the American Lutheran Church North Pacific District Conference and the retirement banquet for our District Bishop Clarence Solberg in 1981, I composed this presentation, which has undergone only modest changes, but I continue to address the subject and collect information on it. The Rev. Matthew Fox's 1979 book on compassion (reprinted 1990) impressed me very much, and my presentation reflects how I was influenced by his views on this important subject.

The past two centuries have been marked by an amazing—yes, a dazzling—progress in science and technology that is without equal in the history of a people. Most of this occurred during my lifetime. It has also been marked by a declared independence from any higher force. Human beings have become the center of everything. Things of the spirit have been abandoned and all that is material has been embraced—and excessively so. The existence of intrinsic evil in people is denied, and the highest existence is the attainment of happiness on earth. At this point, I remind you, if we were born only to be happy, we would not have been born to die. (That's what Solzhenitsyn believes, and I do, too.)

Recently, a university publication came to my office. It described the results of a survey of 350 families conducted by the chairman of a Department of Child and Family Studies. Most of the parents who responded said they would rather have children who are happy and have a strong sense of identity than who are sympathetic to others, tolerant and creative. Everything that fosters the accumulation of material goods and physical well-being is acclaimed—yes, worshipped—today. Materialism is our nation's God. Certainly it fits one of the definitions: "That which makes you anxious in its absence is your God."

We have striven mightily as a nation for human rights, and we need to do more, but in the meantime we have ignored human obligations; we've ignored our inher-

Presented at American Lutheran Church North Pacific Conference, Spokane, Washington, June 13, 1981.

ent responsibilities. Responsibility has essentially faded from the contemporary scene. The unfortunate casualty of the emancipation from the moral heritage of traditional religions with their great reserve of mercy and sacrifice is compassion.

The overwhelming importance of compassion is expressed in the following quotation: "As things are now, it may well be that the survival of the species will depend on the capacity to foster a boundless capacity for compassion.... Compassion alone stands apart from the continuous traffic between good and evil proceeding within us. Compassion is the antitoxin of the soul. Where there is compassion, even the most poisonous impulses remain relatively harmless." (Hoffer, 1980). The person who made this statement is not a theologian; he was a fellow professor in the University of California system when I was there. His name is Eric Hoffer, a longshoreman philosopher. He has a great sense for the feelings of our society. I believe he is right about compassion.

Before I proceed, I must tell you what I believe compassion is. First, I should tell you what it is not. It is not pity, which is feeling sorry for someone. With pity there is condescension and separateness; one does not celebrate with a person one pities. Compassion is suffering with, having empathy with or feelings for. It includes joy as well as grief. It works from a strength born out of shared weakness and an awareness of the mutuality of all living things. The bond is not only between people, but also between people and animals. Compassion is the feeling of togetherness and, therefore, it urges celebration as we forget problems and difficulties. The compassionate person lets go of ego, of individual problems, of personal difficulties in order to remember our common base.

Compassion is not merely feeling or sentiment, but actively helping to relieve pain and suffering in others. A German proverb says that a sorrow shared is a sorrow halved, and a joy shared is a joy doubled. Compassion is a way of living and treating all of life—ourselves (our own body, imagination, dreams and our death), others (both friends and enemies), animals, and our environment. Rabbi Dressner, speaking of the Jewish way of life, stated that compassion was its cornerstone and that mercy was the other side of every act of justice (Fox, 1990).

Two hours before his accidental death, Thomas Merton remarked that the whole idea of compassion is based on awareness of the interdependence of living beings; for they are all part of one another and involved in one another (Fox, 1990). I believe that. In order to develop compassion, we must develop a keener awareness of the interdependence of all living things. This requires study—deep study not only of books and journals, but of nature. It implies that deep study is a means of entering more fully into the pursuit of truth about our universe. It also implies a celebration—a shared joy over the facts about our universe that scientific studies have revealed.

Death of ethical evaluation characterizes sentimentalism. It is easier to believe in something pretty and in sweet-sounding phrases than it is to relate ideas gained from scientific observation to compassion. I say this because there is a rational and an intellectual component to compassion that must not be ignored. Compassion compels us to ask, "Why am I here?" We are here as stewards of earth and all within it, with adequate provision made for future generations. We must develop a reasonable system of sharing, not only across distances, but across time for generations that follow.

Unfortunately, our educational system is programmed to vaccinate us against empathy, against compassion, against working for the common good. The survival values that our society encourages the most are individualistic. We are trained to be cerebral, thick-skinned and obsessed with ourselves. These are not the survival values for a world broken by unshared bread. Unless our generation shows compassion by limiting its share of resources, we are sentencing future generations to deprivation and greater misery.

Matthew Fox (1990) wrote that compassion is the world's richest energy source. Unfortunately, this great energy source remains relatively unused, unexplored and unwanted. In too many places today, compassion has been exiled, as is evident almost everywhere—in a world broken by unshared bread, where 40 percent of our people go to bed hungry every night; in a world broken by racism and loss of a sense of community; in a world broken by the mechanization of medicine where a surprising number of people have no access to adequate medical care or justice; and in a world broken by the proliferation of superfluous luxury.

Today, there are 500-800 million who are starving, including many, many children. The tragedy of it all is that we have the know-how and the wherewithal to relieve this terrible scourge. What we lack is the will and the compassion. Most people are content to do nothing much about it. The response of too many of us is what Ned O'Gorman in Children are Dying called the "abstract calm" of intellectuals and other too-busy people (Fox, 1990). While advocating political change, they live "high-on-the-hog."

Care has many meanings. Often we hear, "I'll take care of him." Commonplace, even innocuous statements that we hear every day tell us much about the mind-set of many people. From the way this sentence is pronounced we know that "taking care of," does not mean showing compassion by our actions. It means getting rid of a nuisance figure, removing a problem. We also learn from some common questions:

"Which car shall we take to the concert?"

"I don't care."

"Do you want to go to the Crescent or the Bon first?"

"I don't care."

"Do you want to have apple or cherry pie for desert?"

"I don't care."

Not to care seems to become more acceptable in our society than to care.

What does it mean to really care? Care has its roots in "Kara," which is a Gothic word meaning to lament, to grieve, to experience sorrow, to cry out. Caring, compassionate people who in our life have meant the most to us are often those who, instead of offering an assortment of advice, cures or solutions, choose to share with us our pain and to touch our hurt with a gentle and tender hand. They are the friends who remain silent and listen to us in moments of despair, who can stay with us in an hour of grief. Such friends join us in acknowledging our own powerlessness when facing death and admitting that they do not understand. They do not encourage us to run away from the pain; they do not busy themselves with trivial tasks, but stand in the face of death together with us as we grieve.

As Henri Nouwen (1974) observed, the friend who cares makes it clear that no matter what happens in the external world, being present to each other is what really matters. In fact, it matters more than pain, illness, or even death. But this is not easy. The temptation is so great to change painful realities immediately, or, failing that, to run away from them. When we cure without care we become controllers and manipulators, unable to form real community. Cure without care makes us preoccupied with quick fixes and makes us impatient and also unwilling to share one another's burdens, unable to experience compassion. Care is more important than cure. In fact, cure without care may be, in the long run, more harmful than helpful.

When one examines compassion and its exile, one is struck with the fact that no one seems to have a corner on either practicing it or rejecting it. Many years ago, Norman Cousins went around the world asking famous people what they had learned in their life. People he questioned included Prime Minister Nehru, Albert Schweitzer, Pope John XXIII and Nikita Krushchev. The last two are particularly relevant as we explore compassion.

Pope John said, "Always learn something new and never hesitate to hold out your hand and never hesitate to accept an outstretched hand." Nikita Krushchev said, "I can give it to you in four words—never turn your back" (Cousins, 1972).

What a contrast in response and in philosophy! You may say that obviously Pope John was a Christian and Krushchev was not. I hasten to remind you that the full horror of places like Belsen or Buchenwald or Dachau, filled with the walking dead (victims which I and some of you witnessed), was engineered by civilized, cultured, Christianized, Western people like us.

William Eckhardt (1973) concluded in his studies that compassion was not consistent with conventional religion as conceived and practiced in our contemporary culture. Compassionate theists (a theist is anyone who believes in God) are in the minority in the Western world today. But Eckhardt did note a connection between compassion and the original teachings of Judaism, Christianity and other great faiths (Fox, 1990).

Unfortunately, religion often has entered into some unholy alliances, usually with empires. Empires, especially expanding ones, often benefit from, and are sustained by, an association with religion. The Constantinian Era of Christianity (A.D. 312-337) may be an example of this. The Church of England during the growth of the British Empire was another one. A visit to St. Paul's Cathedral in London should be very revealing to those who question this supposition. In this great cathedral you can see the tombs of many British generals. If you take time to read the inscriptions, you will learn of their great victories, complete with the number of Indians they killed in each battle. Empires generally do not accommodate compassion, but prefer to exile it (Fox, 1990).

We should seek to make compassion not a religion, but a way of life. It is interesting to note that Christianity, like Judaism, is (and was) really meant to be a way of life, not a religion. Neither Jesus nor the early Christians spoke of Christianity as a religion. I have just finished reading again the Acts of the Apostles, and Christianity is referred to at least seven times as *the way*—never as a religion. An expert on Jewish spirituality stated recently that Christians must learn that Judaism is not a religion but a way of life. Matthew Fox (1990) makes a strong case regarding the difference between a *way* and a *religion*. Fox placed great significance on the fact that Israelites have never been great empire builders—more often than not they have been among the peoples conquered by the empire builders. Recent events, however, are distressing in this regard.

There seems to be a great deal of information indicating that the commitment to religion has, in many cases, taken precedence over a way of living called compassion. Empires, whatever their nature—religious, political, or academic—are threatened by compassionate people. Compassionate people threaten the status quo.

Christianity has exiled compassion for a long time, and in a very insidious way. Compassion has been made sentimental, starting in the Middle Ages (Fox, 1990). What sentimental pity does is to sidetrack the true meaning of compassion. By making it sentimental we destroy compassion, and compassion is divorced from action. The compassion of the Bible resists this. In the Bible, works of mercy are actions, not sentiments. John (I John 3:17-18) addressed this well and pointedly: "If a person who was rich enough in this world's goods saw that one of his brothers or sisters was in need, but closed his heart to this person, how could the love of God be living in him or her? My children, our love is not to be just words or mere talk, but something *real* and active!"

It is well for us to review the corporal works of mercy. The prophet Isaiah (58:6-8) addressed some of them (it is the Lord Yahweh who speaks):

"Is not this the sort of fast that pleases me?
to break unjust fetters and undo the thongs of the yoke,
to let the oppressed go free and break every yoke,
to share your bread with the hungry,
and shelter the homeless poor,
to clothe the man you see to be naked,
and not to turn from your own kin."

Isaiah is talking about actions: feeding the hungry, sheltering the homeless, clothing the naked, and breaking unjust fetters. That's compassion. Sentiments and emotions may be heartfelt and powerful, but in themselves they are not real compassion unless they lead to acts.

There are other remarkable statements in the Bible pertaining to compassionate works. In Isaiah (1:11, 15, 17) are these words: "I do not delight in the blood of bullocks.... When you pray, I will not hear; your hands are full of blood.... Seek justice, relieve the oppressed, do justice for orphans, plead for the widow." Jesus stated about the same things (Matthew 23:23): "Woe unto Scribes and Pharisees, hypocrites. For you tithe mint and anise and cummin and have omitted the weightier matters of the law, justice, mercy and faith." He also said these words: "Go and learn what this means, I desire mercy and not sacrifice" (Matthew 9:13), and in Luke 6:36, "Be ye compassionate as your heavenly Father is compassionate."

It is important for all of us to realize that Jesus not only cured, but he also cared. He had compassion. He did feed the hungry—but He usually received the food from someone else. He shared the sorrow of the widow from Nain before He restored life to her son. He tasted salt with Mary and Martha when their brother Lazarus had died, and He did this before He raised him from the grave.

In the parable of the Good Samaritan, Jesus clearly told what compassion involves: "He had compassion and went to him and bound up his wounds, pouring on oil and wine; then he set him on his own beast and brought him to an inn and took care of him." Look at all those active verbs: *going, binding, pouring, setting, bringing, taking care.* And all of these actions involved taking a risk. This is not just sentiment. This is compassion.

Jesus also spoke of some very specific works of mercy in Matthew 25:

> For I was hungry and you gave me food; I was thirsty and you gave me drink; I was a stranger and you made me welcome; naked and you clothed me, sick and you visited me, in prison and you came to see me....
> I tell you solemnly, in so far as you did this to one of the least of these brothers of mine, you did it to me.

In other words, loving God means helping people who are in pain or in need. Compassionate concern compelled Jesus to feed the hungry, heal the sick, restore those with disabilities, teach the ignorant, and even raise the dead. When people asked him about his mission and his Messiahship, his reply recounted these works of mercy.

And I'm also glad Jesus had great concern for animals. Some of you are no doubt asking what have animals to do with compassion? I wish to discuss this question. First, we *must* be compassionate to animals—and we have some explicit information regarding this subject. It is so very important for everyone to understand that compassion extends to all creation—to the entire universe. "*His compassion* is over all that he made and extends to the lowliest of God's creatures." (Psalms 145:9)

The early Jewish thought emphasized kinship with all creatures. The Sabbath day of rest was for animals as well as people. There is only one interruption of Jewish grace that is permitted and that is if the domestic animals have not been fed. Leo Baeck commented that the Bible placed animals under laws designed for people—an act without parallel in civilization. It is also of great significance to me that according to a Jewish midrash (an exposition of the Hebrew Scriptures), both Moses and David were chosen to lead Israel because of their compassion for animals, a criterion I approve of (Fox, 1990).

According to the Talmud, the Bible teaches that we have a duty to relieve the suffering of animals. Jesus was steeped in these teachings, so it is no surprise that he would direct that the fallen ox be removed from the pit, even on the Sabbath. He frequently used animals for symbols: the lost sheep, the sheep and goats, the birds of the air, the fallen sparrow, fish gathered and not wasted—these in his parables with telling effect. It isn't surprising; he was born in a stable with animals, and that is the way I and others feel we ought to leave this world, in the presence of animals.

There are no Ph.D.s given in compassion (Nouwen, 1974). In a way that is fortunate. It is fortunate because we live in an age of specialists, and whenever there is a problem we call in specialists. If there are problems with your liver or heart or toes, specialists are available for each of them. If you are in need of prayer, if someone has died, or if the world seems to be passing you by or crashing in on you, there are specialists trained to handle these problems. If you don't believe me, I recall for you that during deliberations on the United States Constitution, when things were not going well, Benjamin Franklin suggested opening their sessions with prayer. However, they couldn't because they didn't have any money to hire a chaplain. But for caring, compassion and concern, there are no specialists; they can't be delegated. It is the responsibility of each of us.

Every human being possesses some measure of ability to care, to be compassionate, to listen, to be a friend to someone in need, to touch, to compliment, to say thanks, to hold a hand, to make people laugh, to accept gifts graciously and to taste salt with those who grieve. We all possess these gifts, but they are too often hidden from view. We are too often so busy—by-passing people or animals in need on our way to something or someone that we consider more important. We may not be able to take away the pain, but we can share it.

To illustrate what I mean by compassion I will tell you a few stories. The first one was told to me by a friend, Walter Capps, who is a great scholar and very interested in the contemplative movement. Although he is not a Catholic, he has visited many monasteries, and befriended many monks. One particular monk wished to share with Walter Capps some of his observations. The first one was that he could sit down and write 10 volumes of what is wrong with the Catholic church, and it would all be true. He said he also could sit down and write 20 volumes of what is wrong with America, and it would all be true. But he said, "You know, that takes no talent; what really takes talent is to be generous." That's compassion.

The next story that I want to tell you about is one from the life of Eleanor and Franklin Delano Roosevelt during their White House years. I tell it because Eleanor Roosevelt, whom many people made fun of during her time, was a very compassionate person and history will treat her well. This is the story in the words of Joseph P. Lash, in his book *Eleanor and Franklin* (©1971 by Joseph P. Lash. Reprinted by permission of W.W. Norton & Company, Inc.):

> Among the many letters that she received when she entered the White House was one from a young woman, Bertha Brodsky, who, in wishing her and the President well, added apologetically that she found it difficult to write because her back was crooked and she had to walk "bent sideways." Eleanor immediately replied with words of encouragement.... She sent the letter to the doctor in charge of the Orthopedic Hospital in New York, asking whether a free bed could not be found for Bertha. It was, and when Eleanor came to New York she visited the young woman, who was almost entirely encased in a plaster cast, although her eyes and mouth showed "a determined cheerfulness." The girl came from a very poor Jewish family, her father eking out an existence with a small paper route, and before the visit ended, it was as if Bertha had become one of Eleanor's children. She visited her faithfully and sent flowers regularly. There was a package at Christmas, and flowers were sent to Bertha's mother at Passover. When Bertha was released from the hospital, Eleanor called Pauline Newman of the Women's Trade Union

League, who found a job for her. She also helped Bertha's brother find a job, and when Bertha acquired a serious boyfriend she brought him to Eleanor to have her look him over. Eleanor attended Bertha's wedding, counseled her in moments of early marital strain, and was godmother to her child. "Dear Messenger of God," Bertha addressed her.

Her relationship with Bertha was not untypical. She yearned for situations that imposed duties. She responded to every appeal for help; indeed, sought to anticipate them.... "I do not attempt to judge others by my standards," she said, and she refused to dwell on injury.

That's compassion.

My next story is about Richard; for most of his life, he lived at Bethel in Bielefeld, West Germany. He had cerebral palsy, and spent his entire life flat on his back.

Bethel was started in 1867 when Christians in Westphalia decided that attics and back rooms were not the appropriate places to keep people with mental retardation or epilepsy, so they established a place where these people could come and live together in a community. When I visited there, Bethel had over 5,000 people who were disadvantaged and over 5,000 people taking care of them in some of the most remarkable facilities and under the direction of very enlightened people.

Edna Hong, an American writer, captured the goodness, spirit and mystery of Bethel in a best seller, *Bright Valley of Love* (1976). She and others convinced me of its greatness and that I should visit Bethel. It was very obvious they wanted me to meet Richard when I was there. Richard became very excited when he found out I was American because Americans had helped him in times past. When he found out I was a veterinarian, he became even more excited. He had many questions for me: "Do you ever work on birds? Are you ever able to make them fly again if they have a broken wing? How do you give therapy to fish?" His last question was (after many others), "Do you employ Indians in your College of Veterinary Medicine?" I thought this an unusual question, but since we employ both Native Americans and Indians from India, I could answer yes. Following my taking leave of Richard, I asked my host about this question. Since Native Americans are very popular in Germany, I thought that was what he meant. "No, he meant Indians from India because he's very keen about Indians from India. In fact," he said, "he supports a little child in India." I thought I'd misunderstood him, for how could this person who has been flat on his back all his life support a little child in India. "Well," my host said, "what I didn't tell you is that he has control of his right foot and has learned in recent times to paint very beautiful pictures with his right foot and with the use of mirrors. We sell these pictures and the money goes to support a little child in India." (She is now teaching.)

Richard died on July 13, 1986. He was 62 years old.

I have a picture of Richard painting a picture, and it's on my wall along with some of his paintings. When I think I have a problem, I look at the pictures and my problem pales into insignificance.

The story of Bethel doesn't end with Richard, however. The director of Bethel (and his father before him from 1871 to 1911) were very enlightened directors; they were really geniuses of their time. Fritz von Bodelschwingh, the director, became very concerned when Hitler put out the order that all such people, who were considered less than human, were to be put to death. This would include, of course, all of the patients at Bethel. Fritz refused to fill out the forms, appealed to the high command, but received an unsatisfactory answer. One day Dr. Brandt, Hitler's personal physician, and his associates came to visit Bethel to make arrangements to begin taking Bethel patients. Fritz took Dr. Brandt off to the side and asked him what determined whether a person was less than human. Dr. Brandt said it was their ability to communicate. So Fritz asked him to accompany him to visit their worst cases. This he did. Among those he showed Dr. Brandt was Henrietta who had hydrocephalus, mental retardation and epilepsy. She was asleep when they arrived. Fritz went over to her and stroked her on the head and called her by name. She opened her eyes, saw Fritz, and smiled. He went to see others, probably Otto who knew only a few things in life, but who had a great appreciation for bright colors and food. In fact, Fritz had never seen anyone enjoy food more than Otto.

Fritz knew the patients at Bethel well, and they likewise knew him because he visited them often; he made these frequent visits because he always learned a great deal from the patients. Bethel's philosophy was, and still is: the patients are the professors. After visiting the patients, Fritz finally turned to Dr. Brandt and said, "Although you may not be able to communicate with these people, it is certainly obvious to you that we can communicate with them." With this he turned and walked back to headquarters followed by Dr. Brandt. On arrival back at headquarters, Dr. Brandt told his associates, "We will cease negotiations and return to Berlin."

Although some patients were removed from Bethel, many were saved during the war. They received no help from the government, but provisions were somehow made for them by free-will offerings. They were saved because people with great compassion took time out to listen to those who are hard to listen to. I'm here to tell you that we should all go and do likewise.

I will close with the following story. Hans was a fisherman on the north coast of Norway. Severe storms often struck his area, sometimes with little notice; and so it was late one afternoon. A sudden storm blew up, and a lone fisherman was caught in it. His boat and life were in peril. Word went out to plead for someone to attempt a rescue. Hans unhesitatingly volunteered. He made no inquiries whether someone would pay him for this hazardous rescue attempt and he didn't even ask who it was. He didn't discuss the hazard; he knew about that. It seemed that all that Hans needed to know was that someone was in trouble, and without help they probably would not survive. With great difficulty, and at the risk of his own life, Hans made the rescue. He didn't know until he had completed the rescue that the person whose life he saved was his own brother— and that's the way of compassion.

Everyone who is in need of help is my brother and my sister. That's compassion.

Afterword

Ever since my youth I have always admired, respected and frequently coveted the talent of others. Most attractive to me were those who were blessed with both compassion and talent and applied them in an exemplary way for the benefit of all living beings (and entities, e.g. soil). One of the very exciting aspects of Delta Society meetings is that so many compassionate, talented people from so many disciplines attend and participate. Andrew Rowan, the editor of Anthrozoös, captures this in an editorial (Rowan, 1990) which is reproduced in part here, with some modifications, as a fitting afterword to the papers in this book. And he describes the brainchild of another talented and compassionate person—Bill Balaban— the mastermind and implementer of the Jingles Award program. These award winners, both the people and animals, are also compassionate and talented. I salute them!

The Power Of The Telling Anecdote

The Delta Society...was established to promote service, education, and scientific studies on a wide range of issues dealing with human-animal interaction.... While university scholarship and research are important, objectivity and reason are not necessarily the prime motivators of human activity; it is vital, especially when dealing with animal issues, also to consider compassion and caring. In fact, researchers probably should more actively incorporate the affective aspects of the relationship into their studies because the emotional foundations of a person's interaction with an animal are so central and significant. This was brought home to me emphatically at the 1989 annual conference of the Delta Society in New Jersey.

Delta conferences are generally most enjoyable, offering participants an opportunity to share information and experiences and to build networks with other like-minded individuals. For the academics who participate, I suspect the multidisciplinary nature of the material is a refreshing change from the other meetings they attend; the high "compassion quotient" evident at the Delta meetings may also be attractive.

There are many award functions at these conferences, and the New Jersey meeting was no exception. What was exceptional, however, was the Jingles Award Luncheon.

Editorial published in Delta Society's journal, *Anthrozoös*, 1990, 2(3):140-141. Reprinted with permission.

Jingles was Dr. Boris Levinson's dog and co-therapist. Dr. Levinson wrote two landmark books on animal-assisted therapy (1969, 1972) in which he described how Jingles showed him how to work with an animal co-therapist. In recognition of Jingles' contribution, Bill Balaban, a filmmaker and active supporter of Delta and all it represents, suggested that awards be given to a variety of special therapy animals at each annual Delta conference. For example, an earlier recipient was an assistance dog trained to help a girl plagued with seizures. Remarkably, this dog developed an ability to detect the onset of seizures before either the patient or her family knew that one was about to occur, thus enabling her to live a much more normal life.

At the Jingles Award Luncheon in New Jersey, five animals were honored by their human companions. The first award went to Lemonade, a very gentle and now very old horse, who taught the pleasures of riding to many children and adults suffering from disabilities. Lemonade was the star of a videotape, featuring many endorsements by her alumni and ending with an exuberant birthday party.

The next award winner was an elderly therapy dog who was suffering from cancer. Her owner, a veterinarian, described the dog's very positive attitude to nursing home visitations and her insistence on participating despite the effects of the cancer therapy. At the end, her owner could no longer restrain her tears as she described what the dog meant to her and to the nursing homes she visited.

The next award went to an assistance dog, companion to a person who was on hand to tell us of his dog's activities. This person had been paralyzed in a car accident that had left his wife and children dead. In a motorized wheelchair, he went back to his job as a university teacher. After being robbed three times (and left with his neck broken again), he decided to get a dog. He obtained an assistance animal that became his new family. The dog went with him everywhere— even to swimming competitions (the owner was a medal winner in games for the disabled and the organizer of a swimming team for people with disabilities), where the dog counted and shepherded the others in the team.

The next award went to the guide dog of a young woman who had been blinded when she was in her late teens. The woman talked movingly of the confidence and companionship (not to say new lease on life) that she had gained when she had received her guide dog and of all the activities in which she was now able to participate.

The final award went to a hearing dog. The owner of the dog was a stockman who worked with dairy cows. He stood on the stage and could not speak for about 90 seconds. He then began haltingly, but with increasing confidence, to describe what his dog meant to him. The dog had brought him out of his self-imposed isolation and even learned to identify (by the sound they made) milking machines that were not working properly. The stockman's description of the change his companion had wrought ended when he broke down in tears.

A written description does not begin to match the steady emotional build-up of the awards ceremony. The stories were all poignant and told with sincerity and strength. Even the more cynical of the audience—such as I, who tend to shy away from such functions—could not fail to be moved by the extraordinarily compelling stories and the way each case built on the previous one. However, one could not cite any of the stories as objective proof that animal-assisted therapy works, nor could one use them as case studies to identify factors that are important in explaining human-animal attraction and interaction. But very few people left that luncheon without having their interest in the field, and their wish to help people and animals, reaffirmed in a most powerful way.

....In the face of stories like the five presented at the lunch, it really does not matter what the research data on animal-assisted therapy indicate: The stories, not the cold and unfeeling statistical analyses of variance of research results, will carry the day for most people. From one point of view—that of the concerned scholar intent on identifying the important factors leading to the development of a human-animal bond—this is unfortunate. But, from another perspective, such stories and anecdotes leave our daily life much more interesting and, hopefully, humane.

I do not advocate a life of compassion without reason, nor its opposite—a life of reason without compassion. The latter approach probably causes more suffering than it alleviates while the former does not help deal with systematic problems in our world, nor contribute to the growth of wisdom. It is important for us to learn how to accommodate the telling anecdote in our research on human-animal interactions. We must be scholarly, but we need to be able to engage in scholarship without losing the ability to glory in compassion and love and the warmth and joy gained from animals and nature.

It is appropriate to leave the final words of this editorial to Gerard Manley Hopkins, who captured this wonder when he wrote:

Glory be to God for dappled things—
For skies of couple-colour as a brinded cow;
For rose moles all in stipple upon trout that swim;
Fresh-firecoal chestnut-falls; finches' wings;
Landscape plotted and pieced—fold, fallow, and plough;
And all trades, their gear and tackle and trim.

All things counter, original, spare, strange;
Whatever is fickle, freckled (who knows how?)
With swift, slow; sweet, sour; adazzle, dim;
He fathers-forth whose beauty is past change:
Praise him.

A.N. Rowan
N. Grafton, MA

Appendix

Reverence For Life
Leo K. Bustad and Associates
(Conjoint course: Veterinary Medicine and Philosophy; Variable Credit)

It is the duty of each member of our society to cherish and maintain life, to prevent suffering and to be obedient to a code of ethics that incorporates reverence for life at a time in history marked by mass genocide, extensive human and animal suffering and irresponsible animal and environmental stewardship.

Course Objectives:

1. Write a lucid, documented abstract on one or more subjects related to the human-animal interrelationship and our responsibilities to living things, emphasizing animals.

2. Comprehend the controversial issues relating to animals in the following: Bioethics, grief and the grieving process in people and animals, Judeo-Christian and other religious ethics regarding animals, holocausts and records of people's inhumanity to man and other animals, the human/animal bond, animal-assisted therapy, animal awareness, pain, vegetarianism, controversies relating to animal experimentation and alternatives thereto, animal law and rights, animals in entertainment, cosmetic surgery of animals, euthanizing healthy animals, feeding scarce protein to animals while people are starving, intensive farming and wildlife, endangered species, loss of habitat, population pressures, hunting and trapping, genocide, geocide, phytocide, zoocide, and Schweitzerian philosophy.

3. Identify the critical references and research contributions to the subjects listed in #2.

4. Explain the benefits of animals to each other, to people, and to our environment.

5. Construct an ethical basis for fulfilling your professional responsibilities.

6. Write a detailed outline of a course you would teach on reverence for life.

Course Procedures:

This class will be conducted as a lecture-seminar. Participation is expected by each student, both orally and in writing. Specifically, each participant receiving credit shall:

1. Choose one or more listed topics and make a presentation to the class. An abstract and an annotated bibliography on the topic will be given to the instructor prior to the class presentation.

2. Participate in meaningful discussions of topics presented.

3. Write a brief, helpful analysis of other presentations pointing out the effective aspects, as well as areas that needed more information.

The final examination may consist of an in-class essay relating to content presented in the class. The essay will demonstrate the extent to which the class objectives have been met.

Ethical behavior recognizes and functions within a shared interest. Contrary to the views of many ethical behaviorists, ethics and morals did not have their origins in Christianity or Judaism. It is a matter of history that Greek philosophers were passionately concerned about ethics and morals. Confucius and Taoist teachers built ethical systems independent of the Greek-Hebrew perspective. Near Eastern wisdom and literature was filled with moral teachings before the time of Moses. There is evidence that in the Judeo-Christian tradition, ethics and ethical behavior go well beyond utilitarian considerations into the supreme worth of sacrifice and subordination of self in the service of others, and this extends to animals and our environment. The era of simply having our way with animals and treating them in any manner that suits our fancy and promotes profit is fortunately passing.

Although we have responsibility for animals, disagreement exists over the nature and scope of these responsibilities. Disagreements often occur because of our lack of information regarding the nature of animal mental states, capacities and vulnerabilities. But we know that animals can suffer from loneliness, jealousy, separation, loss, boredom, frustration, rage and pain. If the capability to suffer is a morally relevant characteristic, then the effects determine that animals, as well as people, are proper subjects of moral consideration. It is our duty to help in whatever way we can to improve the quality of animal life. In so doing, animals, animal producers, consumers, and society as a whole can only benefit.

Veterinarians by choice, experience and training are equipped and responsible for relieving suffering in animals; conserving animal resources; preventing, diagnosing, and treating animal diseases; and promoting a healthy human-animal bond. One cannot have a healthy community without a strong human-animal bond. Other professions share in this important responsibility.

Bibliography

Allen, K., and J. Blascovich. 1996. "The Value of Service Dogs for People with Severe Ambulatory Disabilities: A Randomized Controlled Trial." *JAMA* 275(13):1001-1006.

Allen, K., J. Blascovich, J. Tomaka, and R.M. Kelsey. 1991. "Presence of Human Friends and Pet Dogs as Moderators of Autonomic Response to Stress in Women." *Journal of Personal and Social Psychology* 61:582-589.

Altman, P.L., and D.S. Dittmer. 1972 *Biology Data Book.* 2nd ed. Vol. I. Bethesda, MD: Federation of American Societies of Experimental Biology.

Anderson, Maxwell (words) and K. Weill (music). "September Song." From the musical play *Knickerbocker Holiday.* 1988. New York: Crawford Music Corp.

Anderson, R.K., B.I. Hart, and L.A. Hart, eds. 1984. The Pet Connection: *Its Influence on Our Health and Quality of Life.* Minneapolis: CENSHARE, University of Minnesota.

Anderson, R.S. 1975. *Pet Animals in Society.* New York: Macmillan.

Anderson, W.P., C.M. Reid, and G.L. Jennings. 1992. "Pet Ownership and Risk Factors for Cardiovascular Disease." *The Medical Journal of Australia* 157: 298-301.

Arkow, P., ed. 1986. *The Loving Bond: Companion Animals in the Helping Professions.* Saratoga, CA: R & E Publishers.

Arkow, P. 1989. *Pet Therapy: A Study and Resource Guide for the Use of Companion Animals in Selected Therapies.* Colorado Springs, CO: The Humane Society of the Pikes Peak Region.

Ascione, F.R. 1992. "Enhancing Children's Attitudes about the Humane Treatment of Animals: Generalization to Human-Directed Empathy." *Anthrozoös* 5(3):176-191.

Bach, Richard. 1981. Illusions: *The Adventures of a Reluctant Messiah.* New York: Dell.

Barloy, Jean-Jacques. 1978. *Man and Animals:* 100 Centuries of Friendship (trans. by H. Fox). New York: Gordon & Cremonesi.

Barnes, D.M. 1988. "Need for Mother's Touch is Brain-Based." Science 239:142.

Barnett, J.L., G.M. Cronin, P.H. Hemsworth ,and C.G. Winfield. 1984. "The Welfare of Confined Sows: Physiological, Behavioral and Production Responses to Contrasting Housing Systems and Handler Attitudes." *Annales de Recherches Vétérinaires* 15(2):217-226.

Bartolme, J.V., M.B. Bartolme, E.B. Harris, and S.M. Schanberg. 1987. "N Alpha-Acetyl-Beta-Endorphin Stimulates Ornithine Decarboxylase Activity in Preweanling Rat Pups:Opioid- and Non-Opioid-Mediated Mechanisms." *Journal of Pharmacology and Experimental Therapeutics* 240:895-899.

Bartolme, J.V., M.B. Bartolme, E.B. Harris, J.S. Pauk, and S.M. Schanberg. 1989. "Regulation of Insulin and Glucose Plasma Levels by Central Nervous System Beta-Endorphin in Preweanling Rats." *Endocrinology* 124:2153-2158.

Baun, M., N. Bergstrom, N. Langston, and L. Thoma. 1984. "Physiological Effects of Petting Dogs: Influences of Attachment." In *The Pet Connection*, eds. R.K. Anderson, B.L. Hart, and L.A. Hart, pp. 162-170. Minneapolis: CENSHARE, University of Minnesota.

Beck, A.M., and A.N. Rowan. 1994. "The Health Benefits of Human-Animal Interactions." *Anthrozoös* 7(2):85-88.

Beck, A.M., L. Seraydarian, and G.F. Hunter. 1986. "Use of Animals in the Rehabilitation of Psychiatric In-Patients." *Psychology Reports* 58:63-66.

Benjamin, Harold. 1939: *The Saber-Tooth Curriculum.* New York: McGraw-Hill.

Biery, M.J., and N. Kauffman. 1989. "The Effects of Therapeutic Horseback Riding on Balance." *Physical Activity Quarterly* 6:221-229.

Blount, M. 1974. *Animal Land.* New York: Avon.

Bokonyi, S. 1974. *History of Domestic Mammals in Central and Eastern Europe.* Budapest, Hungary: Akademia Kiado.

Bombeck, Erma. 1978. "Are You Listening?" In *If Life Is a Bowl of Cherries, What Am I Doing in the Pits?* New York: McGraw-Hill.

Bonhoeffer, Dietrich. 1964. *Life Together.* London: SCM Press.

Book, S.A., and L.K. Bustad. 1974. "The Fetal and Neonatal Pig in Biomedical Research." *Journal of Animal Science* 38:997-1002.

Bormann, E.G., W.S. Howell, R.G. Nichols, and G.L. Shapiro. 1969. *Interpersonal Communication in the Modern Organization.* Englewood Cliffs, NJ: Prentice Hall.

Bossard, James H.S. 1944. "The Mental Hygiene of Owning a Dog." *Mental Hygiene* 28:408-413.

Bossard, James H.S. 1950. "I Wrote About Dogs: A Mental Hygiene Note." *Mental Hygiene* 34:385-390.

Britt, K. 1978. "The Joy of Pigs." *National Geographic* 154:398-414.

Burke, Edmund. 1989. "Letter to a Member of the French National Assembly." In *The Writings and Speeches of Edmund Burke*, general ed. Paul Langford. vol. 8. Oxford University Press.

Burke, J., S. Daniel, J. Burke, R. Camplone, and C. Tweedy. 1988. "The Effect of a Residential Pet Therapy Program on Isolated Nursing Home Residents." In *Abstracts of Presentations: People, Animals and the Environment: Exploring Our Interdependence.* Delta Society 7th Annual Conference, Sept. 29-Oct. 1, 1988, Orlando, FL. Orlando: Kal Kan.

Bush, Vannevar. 1967. *Science Is Not Enough.* New York: Morrow.

Bustad, Karen Ann. 1985. *Dancing in Africa.* Tacoma, WA: Pacific Lutheran University.

Bustad, L.K. 1966. "Pigs in the Laboratory." *Scientific American* 214:94-100.

Bustad, L.K. 1977. "More Than Scholars." *National Forum* 57(2):13-20.

Bustad, L.K. 1985. "Laboratory Animal Scientists and Their New Role in Human/Animal Bonding." In *The Contribution of Laboratory Animal Science to the Welfare of Man and Animals: Past, Present and Future: 8th Symposium of the International Council for Laboratory Animal Science/Canadian Association for Laboratory Animal Science*, Vancouver, 1983. New York: Fischer Verlag

Bustad, L.K. 1985. "The Importance of Animals to the Well-Being of People." *Trends* 1(5):54-57.

Bustad, L.K. 1987. "Investigator's Interrelationship with Laboratory Animals." In *Effective Animal Care and Use Committees* (special issue of *Laboratory Animal Science*, January 1987) pp. 167-170. Cordova, TN: American Association for Laboratory Animal Science.

Bustad, L.K. 1989. "Editorial: Our Responsibilities to the Natural World." *Anthrozoös* 2:219-220.

Bustad, L.K., and L.M. Hines. 1981. "Human-Companion Animal Bond and the Curriculum." In *Interrelations Between People and Pets*, ed. B. Fogle. Springfield, IL: Charles C.Thomas.

Bustad, L.K., and L.M. Hines. 1984. "Our Professional Responsibilities Relative to Human-Animal Interactions." *Canadian Veterinary Journal* 25:369-376.

Caldwell, Taylor. 1960. *The Listener.* Garden City, NY: Doubleday.

Camus, A. 1966. *Caligula and Three Other Plays.* New York: Knopf.

Caulfield, Catherine. 1984. *In the Rainforest.* Chicago: University of Chicago Press.

Chesterton, G.K. 1961. In *The Symbolic Pig: An Anthology of Pigs in Literature and Art*, eds. F.C. Sellar and R.M. Meyer. Edinburgh: Oliver & Boyd.

Clutton-Brock, J. 1981. *Domesticated Animals From Early Times.* Austin, TX: University of Texas Press.

Conot, R. 1973. *Justice at Nuremberg.* New York: Harper and Row.

Cousins, Norman. 1972. *The Improbable Triumvirate: John F. Kennedy, Pope John, Nikita Krushchev.* New York: W.W. Norton.

Darwin, Sir Francis, 1929. *Autobiography of Charles Darwin.* London: Watts.

Davis, J.H., and McCreary Juhasz, A. 1995. "The Preadolescent/Pet Friendship Bond." *Anthrozoös* 8(2):78-82.

Dismuke, R.P. 1984. "Rehabilitative Horseback Riding for Children with Language Disorders." In *The Pet Connection,* eds. R.K.Anderson, B.L.Hart, and L.A.Hart, pp. 131-140. Minneapolis: CEN-SHARE, University of Minnesota.

Dostoevsky, Feodor. 1912. *The Brothers Karamazov.* New York: Macmillan.

Dostoevsky, Feodor. 1960. *Notes from Underground, and The Grand Inquisitor.* New York: Dutton.

Eckhardt, William. 1973. *Compassion: Toward a Science of Value.* Toronto: CPRI Press.

Eddy, J., L.A. Hart, and R. Boltz. 1988. "The Effects of Service Dogs on Social Acknowledgements of People in Wheelchairs." *Journal of Psychology* 122:39-45.

Eiseley, Loren. 1969. *Unexpected Universe.* New York: Harcourt, Brace and World.

Ensminger, M.E. 1961. *Swine Science.* Danville, IL: The Interstate Printers and Publishers.

Epstein, H., and M. Bichard. 1984. "Pig." In *Evolution of Domesticated Animals.* ed. Ian L. Mason. New York: Longman.

Fogle, Bruce, ed. 1981. *Interrelations Between People and Pets.* Springfield, IL: Charles C. Thomas.

Fogle, Bruce. 1983. *Pets and Their People.* London: Collins Harvill.

Fogle, Bruce. 1986. *Games Pets Play.* London: Michael Joseph.

Fox, Matthew. 1990. *A Spirituality Named Compassion and the Healing of the Global Village, Humpty Dumpty and Us.* San Francisco: Harper. (First published 1979, Minneapolis: Winston Press).

Frank, J.D. 1968. *Sanity and Survival.* NewYork: Vintage Books, Random House.

Frankl, Viktor E. 1963. *Man's Search for Meaning.* New York: Pocket Books.

Friedmann, E., A.H. Katcher, J.J. Lynch, and S.A. Thomas. 1980. "Animal Companions and One-Year Survival of Patients After Discharge from a Coronary Care Unit." *Public Health Report* 95(4):307-312.

Friedmann, E. and S.A. Thomas. 1995. "Pet Ownership, Social Support, and One-Year Survival After Acute Myocardial Infarction in the Cardiac Arrhythmia Suppression Trial (CAST)." *American Journal of Cardiology* 76:1213-1217.

Ginott, Haim G. 1972. *Teacher and Child.* New York: Macmillan.

Gross, W.B., and P.B. Siegel. 1982. "Socialization as a Factor in Resistance to Infection, Feed Efficiency and Response to Antigen in Chickens." *American Journal of Veterinary Research* 43:2010-2012.

Halberstam, David. 1971. *The Best and the Brightest.* New York: Random House.

Haley, Alex. 1976. *Roots.* Garden City, NY: Doubleday.

Hammet, F.S. 1921. "Studies on the Thyroid Apparatus." *Amercan Journal of Physiology* 56:196-204.

Hart, L.A., B. Hart, and B. Bergin. 1987. "Socializing Effects of Service Dogs for People with Disabilities." *Anthrozoös* 1(1):41-44.

Hart, L.A., B. Hart, and B. Mader. 1985. "Effects of Pets in California Governmentally-Assisted Housing for the Elderly." *Journal of the Delta Society* 1:65-66.

Hedgepeth, W. 1978. *The Hog Book.* Garden City: Doubleday.

Hemsworth, P.H., J.L. Barnett, and C. Hansen. 1981. "The Influence of Handling by Humans on the Behavior, Growth and Corticosteroids in the Juvenile Female Pig." *Hormone Behavior* 15:398-403.

Hendy, H.M. 1984. "Effects of Pets on the Sociability and Health Activities of Nursing Home Residents." In *The Pet Connection,* eds. R.K. Anderson, B.L. Hart, and L.A.Hart, pp. 430-437. Minneapolis: CENSHARE, Universityof Minnesota.

Hines, D.M., ed. 1976. *Tales of the Okanogans*. Fairfield, WA: Ye Galleon Press.

Hoffer, Eric. 1980. "The Human Factor in Science, Technology and the Human Prospect." In *Procedings of the Edison Centennial Symposium*, eds. C. Starr and P.C. Rittterbush. New York: Pergamon.

Holcomb, R., and M. Meacham. 1989. "Effectiveness of an Animal-Assisted Therapy Program in an Inpatient Psychiatric Unit." *Anthrozoös* 2(4):259-264.

Hong, Edna. 1976. *Bright Valley of Love*. Minneapolis: Augsburg Publishing House.

Hooper, Walter. 1982. *Through Joy and Beyond*. New York: Macmillan.

House, J.S., K.R. Landis, and D. Umberson. 1988. "Social Relationships and Health." *Science* 241:540-545.

Hudson, William Henry. 1919. "My Friend the Pig." In *The Book of a Naturalist*. New York: George H. Soran.

Hunt, S.J., L.A. Hart, and R. Gomulkiewicz. 1992. "The Role of Small Animals in Social Interactions between Strangers." *Journal of Social Psychology* 132(2):245-256.

Hutton, J.S. 1985. "A Study of Companion Animals in Foster Families: A Perception of Therapeutic Values in the Human-Pet Relationship." In *The Human-Pet Relationship: International Symposium on the Occasion of the 80th Birthday of Nobel Prize Winner Prof. Dr. Konrad Lorenz, Oct. 27-28, 1983*, pp. 64-70. Vienna: Austrian Academy of Sciences, Institute for Interdisciplinary Research on the Human-Pet Relationship.

Institute for Interdisciplinary Research on the Human-Pet Relationship (IIRHPR). 1985. *The Human-Pet Relationship: International Symposium on the Occasion of the 80th Birthday of Nobel Prize Winner Prof. Dr. Konrad Lorenz, Oct. 27-28, 1983*. Vienna.

International Therapeutic Riding Congress (ITRC), 6th, August 23-27 1988, Toronto. 1988. *6th International Therapeutic Riding Congress*. Thornhill, Ontario, Canada: The Congress.

Jones, Harold E. 1923. *Experimental Studies of College Training: The Effect of Examination on Permanence of Learning*. (Archives of Psychology No. 68) New York: Columbia University.

Kase, Colette. 1996. "Pets and Housing—The Benefits and the Need: Update on Current Situation." Report delivered at the Conference on Making Space for Pets: Health and Social Benefits, London, March 27.

Katcher, A.H. 1981. "Interactions Between People and Their Pets: Form and Function." In *Interrelations Between People and Pets*, ed. Bruce Fogle. Springfield, IL: Charles C. Thomas.

Katcher, A.H. 1987. "Health and Caring for Living Things." *Anthrozoös* 1(3):175-183.

Katcher, A.H. 1988. "The Evolution of Human Affection: The Significance of the Living Environment in the Modern World." In *Abstracts of Presentations: People, Animals and the Environment: Exploring Our Interdependence*. Delta Society 7th Annual Conference, Sept. 29-Oct. 1, 1988, Orlando, FL. Orlando: Kal Kan.

Katcher, A.H. and A. Beck, eds. 1983. *New Perspectives on Our Lives with Companion Animals*. Philadelphia: University of Pennsylvania Press.

Katcher, A.H., A. Beck, E. Friedmann, and J. Lynch. 1983. "Looking, Talking and Blood Pressure: The Physiological Consequences of Interaction with the Living Environment." In *New Perspectives on Our Lives with Companion Animals*, eds. A. Katcher and A. Beck, pp. 351-359. Philadelphia: University of Pennsylvania Press.

Katcher, A.H., A. Beck, and D. Levine. 1989. "Evaluation of a Pet Program in Prison." *Anthrozoös* 2(3):175-180.

Katcher, A.H., H. Segal, and A.M. Beck. 1984. "Comparison of Contemplation and Hypnosis for the Reduction of Anxiety and Discomfort During Dental Surgery." *American Journal of Clinical Hypnosis* 27:14-21.

Kaye, D.M. 1984. "Animal Affection and Student Behavior." In *The Pet Connection*, eds. R.K. Anderson, B.L. Hart, and L.A. Hart, pp.101-104. Minneapolis: CENSHARE, University of Minnesota.

Kidd, A.H., and R.M. Kidd. 1994. "Benefits and Liabilities of Pets for the Homeless." *Psychological Reports* 74:715-722.

Kundera, Milan. 1984. *The Unbearable Lightness of Being.* New York: Harper and Row.

Kushner, Harold. 1989. *When Bad Things Happen to Good People.* 2nd ed. New York: Schocken Books.

Levinson, Boris M. 1969. *Pet-Oriented Child Psychology.* Springfield, IL.: Charles C. Thomas.

Levinson, Boris M. 1972. *Pets and Human Development.* Springfield, IL.: Charles C. Thomas.

"Life-Saving Pig Receives Stillman Award." 1985. *Advocate* 3(1):16.

Lilje, Hanns. 1950. *The Valley of the Shadow* (trans. Olive Wyon). Philadelphia: The Muhlenberg Press.

Lynch, J.J. 1977. *The Broken Heart: The Medical Consequences of Loneliness.* New York: Basic Books.

Mader, B., and L.A. Hart. 1989. "Social Acknowledgements for Children with Disabilities: Effects of Service Dogs." *Child Development* 60:1529-1534.

Mellen, I.M. 1952. *The Natural History of the Pig.* New York: Exposition Press.

Melson, G.F. 1990. "Fostering Inter-connectedness with Animals and Nature: The Developmental Benefits for Children." *People, Animals, Environment* 8(4):15-17.

Melson, G.F., E.O. Strimple, and L.K. Bustad. 1993. "The Benefits of Interactions of Children and Animals." In *Healthy Children 2000: Obstacles and Opportunities: Proceedings of the Fourth National Policy Forum, April 24-25, 1992,* pp.142-147. Washington: National Academies of Practice.

Mendelsohn, E. 1973. "A Human Reconstruction of Science." *Barton University Journal* (Spring):45-52.

Montagu, Ashley. 1971. *Touching: The Human Significance of the Skin.* New York: Columbia University Press. (2nd Ed. 1978. New York: Harper & Row.)

Nielsen, J.A., and L. Delude. 1989. "Behavior of Young Children in the Presence of Different Kinds of Animals." *Anthrozoös* 3(2):119-129.

Nichols, R.G., and L.A. Stevens. 1957. *Are You Listening?* New York: McGraw-Hill.

Nouwen, Henri J.M. 1974. *Out of Solitude: Three Mediations on the Christian Life.* Notre Dame IN: Ave Maria Press.

Patronek, G.J. 1995. "Development and Validation of an Ecological Model for Describing the Pet Dog Population in the United States and an Epidemiologic Study of Risk Factors for an Owner's Failure to Retain Their Dog as Pets in the Home." Ph.D. thesis, Purdue University.

Patronek G.J., and L.T. Glickman. 1994. "Development of a Model for Estimating the Size and Dynamics of the Pet Dog Population." *Anthrozoös* 7(1):25-42.

Patronek, G.J., and A.N. Rowan. 1995. "Editorial: Determining Dog and Cat Numbers and Population Dynamics." *Anthrozoös* 8(4):199-205.

Pauk, J., C.M. Kuhn, T.M. Field, and S.M. Schanberg. 1986. "Positive Effects of Tactile Versus Kinesthetic or Vestibulal Stimulation on Neuroendocrine and ODC Activity in Maternally-Deprived Rat Pups." *Life Sciences* 39:2081-2087.

Peacock, C.A. 1984. *The Role of the Therapist's Pet in Initial Psychotherapy Sessions with Adolescents: An Exploratory Study.* Ph.D. thesis, Boston College.

Peddiwell, J.A., pseudonym. See: Benjamin, Harold.

Pope, Alexander. 1843. *Essay on Man.* Boston: W.B. Fowle and N. Capen.

Raines, Robert A. 1966. *Creative Brooding.* New York: Macmillan.

Rankin, Paul T. 1930. "Listening Ability: Its Importance, Measurement and Development." *Chicago Schools Journal* 12:177-179, 417-420.

Robb, S.S. 1987. "Summary of Health Benefits of Pets for Elderly Residents in Health Care Centers." Presentation at National Institutes of Health Technology Assessment Workshop on Health Benefits of Pets, Sept. 10-11, Bethesda, MD.

Robinson, Michael H. 1988. "Zoos Today and Tomorrow." *People, Animals, Environment* 6(1) 29-32.

Robinson, Michael H. 1988a. "Bioscience Education Through Bioparks." *BioScience* 38:630-634.

Robinson, Michael H. 1989. "What Are Our Responsibilities to the Natural World: Should We Save the Rain Forests?" *Anthrozoös* 2:221-235.

Ross, S., M.G. Vigdor, M. Kohnstamm, M. DiPaoli, B. Manley, and L. Ross. 1984. "The Effects of Farm Programming with Emotionally Handicapped Children." In *The Pet Connection,* eds. R.K. Anderson, B.L. Hart, and L.A. Hart. Minneapolis: CENSHARE, University of Minnesota.

Ross, S.B. Jr. 1981. "Children and Companion Animals." *Ross Timesaver: Feelings and Their Medical Significance* 23(4):13-16.

Roughgarden, J. 1989. "The United States Needs an Ecological Survey." *BioScience* 39(1):5.

Rowan, A.N. 1990. "Editorial: The Power of the Telling Anecdote." *Anthrozoös* 3(3):140-141.

Rowan, A.N., ed. 1988. *Animals and People Sharing the World*. Hanover, NH: University Press of New England.

Saint Exupéry, Antoine de. 1943. *The Little Prince*. New York: Harcourt, Brace and World.

Sato, S., K. Tarumizu, and K. Hatae. 1993. "The Influence of Social Factors on Allogrooming in Cows." *Applied Animal Behaviour Science* 38:235-244.

Schanberg, S.M, and T.M. Field. 1987. "Sensory Deprivation Stress and Supplemental Stimulation in the Rat Pup and Preterm Human Neonate." *Child Development* 58:1431-1447.

Schweitzer, Albert. 1923. *Civilization and Ethics* (trans. by J. Naish). London: A & C Black.

Schweitzer, Albert. 1953. *Out of My Life and Thought: An Autobiography*. New York: New American Library.

Schweitzer, Albert. 1970. *Reverence for Life*. London: S.P.C.K.

Serpell, J. 1991. "Beneficial Effects of Pet Ownership on Some Aspects of Human Health and Behaviour." *Journal of the Royal Society of Medicine* 84:717-720.

Siegel, J.M. 1990. "Stressful Life Events and Use of Physician Services Among the Elderly: The Moderating Role of Pet Ownership." *Journal of Personality and Social Psychology* 58(6):1081-1086.

Siegel, J.M. 1993. "Companion Animals: In Sickness and in Health." *Journal of Social Issues*, 49:157-167.

Siegel, J.M. 1995. "Pet Ownership and the Importance of Pets Among Adolescents." *Anthrozoös* 8(4): 217-223.

Solzhenitsyn, Aleksandr. 1963. *One Day in the Life of Ivan Denisovich*. New York: Bantam.

Solzhenitsyn, Aleksandr. 1974. *The Gulag Archipelago*. New York: Harper and Row.

Stallones, L. 1990. "Companion Animals and Health of the Elderly." *People, Animals, Environment* 8(4):18-19.

Styron, William. 1979. *Sophie's Choice*. New York: Random House.

Towne, C.W., and E.N. Wentworth. 1950. *Pigs from Cave to Corn Belt*. Norman, OK: University of Oklahoma Press.

Valentine, D.P., M. Kiddoo, and B. LaFleur. 1993. "Psychosocial Implications of Service Dogs for People Who Have Mobility or Hearing Impairments." *Social Work and Health Care* 19:109-125.

Van de Castle, R.L. 1983. "Animal Figures in Fantasy and Dreams." In *New Perspectives on Our Lives With Companion Animals*, eds. A. Katcher and A. Beck. Philadelphia: University•of Pennsylvania Press.

Vaughan, S., L. Peterson, L.K. Bustad, T.D. Ryan, and L.M. Hines. 1986. *Learning and Living Together: Building the Human-Animal Bond*. Pullman, WA: People-Pet Partnership, Washington State University College of Veterinary Medicine.

Vaughn, J.H. 1989. "Conservation in Latin America: A Personal View." *Tropicus* 1(Spring):6.

Vonnegut, Kurt Jr. 1961. *Mother Night*. New York: Avon.

Walsh, P.G., and P.G. Mertin. 1994. "The Training of Pets as Therapy Dogs in a Women's Prison: A Pilot Study." *Anthrozoös*. 7(2): 124-128.

Wilson, C.C. 1991. "The Pet as an Anxiolytic Intervention." *Journal of Nervous and Mental Disease* 179:482-489.

Wilson, E.O. 1989. "Threats to Biodiversity." *Scientific American* 261(3):108-116.

Youatt. W., and S. Sidney 1860. *The Pig*. London: Routledge Warne & Routledge.

About The Author

*L*eo K. Bustad is professor and former dean of the College of Veterinary Medicine at Washington State University. He holds three degrees from Washington State University: a B.S. in agriculture, an M.S. in animal nutrition, and a D.V.M. (Doctor of Veterinary Medicine). He received a Ph.D. in physiology from the University of Washington School of Medicine. For 16 years, he was an employee of General Electric Company and he spent 8 years at the University of California, Davis, where he was a lab director and a professor at UCD's Schools of Medicine and Veterinary Medicine.

Dr. Bustad holds or has held committee assignments and council positions in and served as consultant to many national organizations, both governmental and private. He served as a consultant to the Surgeon General of the U.S. Air Force.

Dr. Bustad has published extensively on education, energy, nutrition, radiation, cancer, laboratory animal medicine, comparative medicine, and the human-companion animal bond. His book *Animals, Aging and the Aged* was published by the University of Minnesota. More recently he coauthored the handbook *Learning and Living Together: Building the Human-Animal Bond*. He has been a national and world leader in the involvement of animals to help people, especially those who are elderly or have handicaps.

He has been a visiting professor at Murdoch University in Western Australia, University of Washington School of Medicine, University of Georgia, Pacific Lutheran University, University of Tennessee, University of Illinois, and Louisiana State University.

The Veterinary Science Building at Washington State University was named for him. He is a member of the National Academies of Practice. He is President Emeritus of Delta Society and Director of the People-Pet Partnership program, Washington State University.

He is the 20th recipient of Washington State University's highest honor, the Regents' Distinguished Alumnus Award. He is a senior member of the Institute of Medicine of the National Academy of Sciences.

In 1991, in Vienna, Austria, he was presented with the World Small Animal Veterinary Association Prize for service to the profession.

In 1995 he receive the American Veterinary Medical Association President's Award in recognition of his contributions to the profession and of his efforts to create greater public and professional awareness and understanding of the Human-Animal Bond and the People-Pet Partnership.

He was selected as the recipient of the American Animal Hospital Association's 1996 WALTHAM Award. This award is given in recognition of outstanding public service activities by a veterinarian, resulting in the improvement of the well-being of companion animals in the world veterinary community.

Also in 1996, he and Bridget were chosen as inaugural members of the *Dog Fancy* Hall of Fame.

Selected Published Presentations By Leo K. Bustad

1. Bustad, L.K. 1976. "Freedom: Facing up to our Responsibilities." *View Northwest* February:40-42.

2. Bustad, L.K. 1976. "Pets for People Therapy." *Western Vet* 14(2):28-31.

3. Bustad, L.K. 1977. "More Than Scholars." *Phi Kappa Phi Journal* (Spring):13-20.

4. Bustad, L.K. 1978. "Pets for People Therapy." *Today's Animal Health* 9(5):8-10.

5. Bustad, L.K. 1979. "Animals' Contribution to Making People Human and Humane." In *Proceedings of the Second Canadian Symposium on Pets and Society*. Vancouver, BC: Canadian Veterinary Medical Association and the Canadian Federation of Humane Societies.

6. Bustad, L.K. 1979. "How Animals Make People Human and Humane." *Modern Veterinary Practice* 60(9):707-710.

7. Bustad, L.K. 1979. "The Peripatetic Dean: People-Pet Partnership." *Western Vet* 17(3):2-4.

8. Bustad, L.K. 1979. "The Peripatetic Dean: Profiling Animals for Therapy." *Western Vet* 17(1): 2.

9. Bustad, L.K. 1979. "The Peripatetic Dean: Veterinary Medicine's Responsibilities to the Handicapped." *Western Vet* 17(2):2.

10. Bustad, L.K. 1980. "The Veterinarian and Animal-Facilitated Therapy." In *Proceedings of the American Animal Hospital Association*. South Bend, IN.

11. Bustad, L.K., and L.M. Hines. 1981. "A Curriculum to Promote Greater Understanding of the Human/Companion Animal Bond." In *Interrelations Between People and Pets*, ed. Bruce Fogle. Springfield, IL: Charles C. Thomas.

12. Bustad, L.K., and L.M. Hines. 1981. "Animal Contributions to the Health and Well-Being of People, Especially the Aging." In *Proceedings of the Inaugural Seminar of the Joint Advisory Committee on Pets in Society*. Melbourne, Victoria, Australia.

13. Bustad, L.K., L.M. Hines, and J.A. Rimbach. 1982. "The Bond Between People and Their Animal Companions." *Animals* 11 Spring issue.

14. Bustad, L.K., and L.M. Hines. 1982. "People and Pets: A Positive Partnership." In *Proceedings of 3rd Symposium, Pets in Society: The Social Importance of Pets in an Aging Society*. Toronto, Canada.

15. Bustad, L.K., and L.M. Hines. 1982. "Placement of Animals with the Elderly: Benefits and Strategies." *California Veterinarian* 8:37-50.

16. Bustad, L.K. 1983. "Dean's Responsibility and Bioethics." *Journal of Veterinary Medical Education* 9(3):97-98.

17. Bustad, L.K. 1983. "Impact of History, Literature and Art on Teaching Reverence for Life." *Journal of Veterinary Medical Education* 9(3):83-87.

18. Bustad, L.K., and L.M. Hines. 1983. "Placement of Animals with the Elderly: Benefits and Strategies." In *New Perspectives on Our Lives with Companion Animals*. A.H. Katcher and A.M. Beck, eds. Philadelphia, PA: University of Pennsylvania Press.

19. Bustad, L.K., and L.M. Hines, 1984. "The Human-Animal Bond: Historical Perspectives." In *The Pet Connection: Its Influence on Our Health and Quality of Life*. R.K. Anderson, B.L. Hart, L.A. Hart, eds. Minneapolis: CENSHARE, University of Minnesota.

20. Bustad, L.K., and L.M. Hines, 1984. "Our Role in the Human/Animal Bond and Promotion of Human Health and Well-Being." In *Proceedings of the XXII World Veterinary Congress.* Perth, Western Australia.

21. Bustad, L.K., and L.M. Hines, 1984. "Our Professional Responsibilities Relative to Human/Animal Interactions." *Canadian Veterinary Journal* 25:369-376.

22. Bustad, L.K. 1985. "Symposium Summary." In The *Human-Pet Relationship: International Symposium on the Occasion of the 80th Birthday of Nobel Prize Winner Prof. Dr. Konrad Lorenz.* Vienna, Austria: Austrian Academy of Sciences, Institute for Interdisciplinary Research on the Human-Pet Relationship.

23. Bustad, L.K. 1985. "The Importance of Animals to the Well-Being of People." *Trends* 1(5):54-57.

24. Bustad, L.K., and R.K. Anderson. 1985. "Preface." In *Vet Clinics: The Human-Companion Animal Bond,* V. Voith and J. Quackenbush, eds. Philadelphia: Saunders.

25. Bustad, L.K. 1986. "The Human-Animal Bond and Reverence for Life." In *Proceedings of the American Minor Breeds Conservancy* Sept. 24-29.

26. Bustad, L.K., and L.M. Hines, guest editors. 1986. "Animals in Society." *National Forum.*

27. Bustad, L.K., and L.M. Hines. 1986. "Compassion for Animals." *National Forum* 66:2-3.

28. Hines, L.M., and L.K. Bustad. 1986. "Historical Perspectives on Human-Animal Interactions." *National Forum* 66:4-6.

29. Vaughan, S., L. Peterson, L.K. Bustad, T.D. Ryan, and L.M. Hines. 1986. *Learning and Living Together: Building the Human-Animal Bond.* Pullman, WA: People-Pet Partnership, Washington State University College of Veterinary Medicine.

30. Bustad, L.K. 1987. "An Historic Perspective of Veterinary Medical Education." *Journal of Veterinary Medical Education* 14(2):38-43.

31. Bustad, L.K. 1988. "Living Together: People, Animals, Environment—A Personal Historical Perspective." *Perspectives in Biology and Medicine* 31(2):171

32. Bustad, L.K., and L.M. Hines, 1988. "The Human-Animal Bond: Our Profession's Responsibilities." In *Proceedings of the XXIII World Veterinary Congress.* Montreal, Canada.

33. Bustad, L.K. 1988. "Our Profession's Responsibilities Regarding the Living Bond: People, Animals, Environment." *Intervet* March 10,11,14.

34. Bustad, L.K. 1989. "Man and Beast Interface. An Overview of Our Relationships." In *Man and Beast Revisited,* eds. M. Robinson and L. Tiger. Smithsonian Press.

35. Bustad, L.K. 1989. "Editorial: Our Responsibilities to the Natural World." *Anthrozoös* 2:219-220.

36. Bustad, L.K. 1989. "Delta Society and Health Benefits and Animals." *Animal: Magazine of Natural History* 2:197.

37. Bustad, L.K. 1989. "People-Animal Interaction. A Look Back—A Look Ahead." *Companion Animal Practice* 19:30-33.

Unpublished Presentations By Leo K. Bustad

1. "The Inner Ring." Senior Banquet, College of Veterinary Medicine, Pullman, WA, June 1974.

2. "My General Philosophy." February 1975.

3. "What It's Like to be Really Hungry." World Hunger Symposium, Pullman, WA, May 1981.

4. "Maintaining Human and Humane Values in a Technological World." Computer Applications in Veterinary Medicine Conference at Mississippi State University, October 1982.

5. "Reverence for Life." Danforth Regional Conference. Pullman, WA, April 1984.

6. "Death and Grief and Its Relief." California Veterinary Medical Association, San Diego, CA, November 1986.

7. A Group of Short Papers Recalling Special Days:
   National P.O.W. Day
   Invasion of Normandy
   Armistice Day

8. "Understanding the Interaction of People, Animals and the Environment." 10th Annual Convention of the Japanese Animal Hospital Association, July 1988.

9. "Therapeutic Aspects of the Human-Animal Bond: Yesterday, Today and Tomorrow." 10th Annual Convention of the Japanese Animal Hospital Association, July 1988.

10. "Health Benefits of Animals." Annual Convention of the American Veterinary Medical Association, Portland, OR, July 1988.

11. "The Health Benefits of Cats." Press conference sponsored by the German Cat Lovers Society in Amsterdam, November 1988.

12. "Health Benefits of Human-Animal Interaction." International Llama Association Conference in Salt Lake City, UT, June 1989.

Honors And Awards

Borden Award, Highest Scholarship in Veterinary Medicine, 1949

National Science Foundation Postdoctoral Fellow, 1958

John Gunion Rutherford Memorial Lecture in Comparative Medicine, University of Saskatchewan, 1979

LaCroix Memorial Lecture, American Animal Hospital Association, 1980

Veterinarian of the Year in Washington State, 1980

Sir William Weipers Lecture, University of Glasgow, 1982

Visiting Professor, Murdoch University, Australia, 1983

Invited address, plenary session of the World Veterinary Congress, Perth, Australia, 1983

Visiting Professor, University of Washington School of Medicine, 1983

Visiting Distinguished Bicentennial Professor, University of Georgia, 1984

Award of Merit, American Animal Hospital Association, 1984

Old Master, Purdue University, 1984

Distinguished Service Award, Washington State Veterinary Medical Association, 1984

Veterinary Science Building renamed Bustad Hall, 1985

Professor D.L.T. Smith Memorial Lecture, University of Saskatchewan, 1985

Dr. John O'Donoghue Memorial Lecture, University of Alberta, 1985

Bustad Companion Animal Veterinarian of the Year Award, sponsored by American Veterinary Medical Association, Delta Society, and Hill's Pet Products, established 1985

Visiting Professor, Pacific Lutheran University, 1986

Visiting Professor, University of Tennessee, 1986

Miller Visiting Professor, University of Illinois, 1987

Elected to National Academies of Practice, 1987

WSU Alumni Achievement Award, 1987

Regent's Distinguished Alumni Award (Washington State University's highest award), 1987

Invited Address, Plenary Session, World Veterinary Congress, Montreal, 1987

Visiting Professor, Louisiana State University and University of Tennessee, 1988

Elected to Senior membership in the Institute of Medicine of the National Academy of Sciences, 1988

Keynote address for the Japanese Animal Hospital Association, Tokyo, 1988

Delta Society Distinguished Service Award, 1990

World Small Animal Veterinary Association Prize, Vienna, 1991

American Veterinary Medical Association President's Award, 1995

American Animal Hospital Association's WALTHAM Award, 1996

For More Information

Delta Society

People have long been intrigued by the complex emotional relationships between people and animals. Today, an impressive number of studies demonstrates the incredible benefits that result from these special relationships. Delta is a human service organization that transforms this growing body of scientific information into practical applications for everyday life.

Delta's mission is to promote animals helping people improve their health, independence and quality of life. We do this by:
- Expanding awareness of the positive effects animals can have on family health and human development.
- Reducing barriers to involvement of animals in everyday life.
- Delivering animal-assisted therapy to more people.
- Increasing the availability of well-trained service dogs.

Delta Programs and Services:

Pet Partners® Program/Animal-Assisted Therapy Services
Helping people heal through interactions with specially trained pets
National Service Dog Center™
Assisting people with disabilities to achieve greater independence and surmount barriers in their environment through service dogs
People and Pets
Teaching individuals and families how companion animals improve health and well-being in everyday life
Publications
Newsletters, quarterly magazine, and scientific journal for professionals, volunteers and the general public
Delta Society is a 501(c)3 tax exempt organization incorporated in the State of Washington.
Headquarters: 289 Perimeter Road East, Renton, WA 98055-1329; tel. 206-226-7357, ActionLine 1-800-869-6898 (voice) 1-800-809-2714 (TDD)
email: deltasociety@cis.compuserve.com
website: http://www.deltasociety.org

The People-Pet Partnership

The People-Pet Partnership (PPP), headquartered at Washington State University, is a nonprofit organization providing four community service programs: the Pet Education Partnership for the teaching of animal awareness and responsible pet ownership to elementary school children; the Companion Animal Partnership which provides resident pets and animal visitation programs for area long-term care facilities, mental health centers, and hospitals; Partnership in Equine Therapy and Education, a therapeutic horseback riding program for people with emotional, physical, and mental disabilities; and the Pet Loss Partnership which provides support for those people who have lost their animal companions.

Complete copies of selected unpublished presentations by Leo K. Bustad, PPP brochures, and the handbook *Learning and Living Together: Building the Human-Animal Bond* are available from PPP. Send a stamped, self-addressed envelope for copies of presentations. For more information contact:

People-Pet Partnership
College of Veterinary Medicine
Washington State University
P.O. Box 647010
Pullman, WA 99164-7010

Additional copies of this book can be ordered from Delta Society